salads
& dressings

salads
& dressings
simple recipes for delicious food every day

rps

LONDON · NEW YORK

Designer Paul Stradling

Production Manager Gary Hayes

Art Director Leslie Harrington

Editorial Director Julia Charles

Indexer Hilary Bird

First published in 2013
by Ryland Peters & Small
20–21 Jockey's Fields
London WC1R 4BW
and
519 Broadway, 5th Floor
New York NY 10012

www.rylandpeters.com

Text © Tamsin Burnett-Hall, Maxine
Clark, Liz Franklin, Tonia George, Brian
Glover, Dunja Gulin, Fiona Smith and
Ryland Peters & Small 2013

Design and photographs © Ryland
Peters & Small 2013

ISBN: 978-1-84975-376-0

10 9 8 7 6 5 4 3 2 1

A CIP record for this book is available
from the British Library.

US Library of Congress Cataloging-in-
Publication data has been applied for.

Printed and bound in China

notes:

• All spoon measurements are level, unless otherwise specified.

All herbs used in these recipes are fresh, unless otherwise specified.

• All fruit and vegetables should be washed thoroughly before consumption. Unwaxed citrus fruits should be used whenever possible.

• All eggs are medium UK/large US, unless otherwise specified. Recipes containing raw or partially cooked egg should not be served to the very young, very old, anyone with a compromised immune system or pregnant women.

contents

not just greens...

Everyone loves a salad. It's one of the world's most versatile dishes. You can serve something small, light and elegant as an appetizer, something substantial and satisfying as a main course or something contrasting and crunchy as a side dish to simply prepared foods.

It's odd to think that the word is derived from the Latin *sal* (salt). The Romans ate vegetables and leaves with a simple dressing of salt, oil or vinegar – similar to the way they still do today, in dishes like *pinzimonio* (crudités with vinaigrette). That may be why we identify dishes dressed with these three items as 'salads' when they appear in other cuisines. The Japanese serve *aemono* and *sunomono*, or 'little vinegared things', in tiny, elegant bowls. The Vietnamese have a passion for huge plates of herbs, 'table salads', which are added to many dishes. A true Vietnamese salad – or one from other countries in the region – is often dressed with fish sauce (the salt element) and lime juice (the vinegar element).

This book gives you a taste of salads from all around the world. The familiar classics are included, along with plenty of new ideas to try. There are light summer salads, warm salads for winter and plenty of ideas for inspired side salads, suitable for serving as part of a party buffet or a barbecue spread.

The key to any great salad is using good quality fresh ingredients and remember that a dressing can make or break a recipe. With that in mind, in addition to the complete recipes, there follow some simple ideas for a variety of dressings that take their inspiration from different world cuisines – from classic vinaigrettes and mayonnaises to Asian and Japanese dressings. Be inspired to try these with your own favourite combinations of salad ingredients to create new favourites.

the vinaigrette family

Vinaigrette can be a simple thing – just oil, vinegar or other acidulator such as lime or lemon juice, plus salt and freshly ground black pepper. You can add other ingredients to ring the changes, but this simple mixture can't be beaten. The oil should be as good as you can find, and the vinegar as little as possible. The secret is in the ratio of oil to vinegar. Start with a ratio of 6 parts oil to 1 part vinegar, and adjust to suit your personal taste. A few pointers – you might need more oil if you use lemon juice rather than vinegar and if you have to add sugar, you've probably used too much vinegar.

Classic vinaigrette

6 tablespoons extra virgin olive oil
1 tablespoon white wine vinegar
sea salt and freshly ground
black pepper

Makes about 125 ml/½ cup

Put the oil, vinegar, salt and pepper in a salad bowl and beat with a fork or small whisk.

Variations

• Add 1 teaspoon Dijon mustard and beat well. The mustard helps form an emulsion.
• Use spicy Moroccan harissa paste instead of mustard.
• Crush the garlic with a pinch of salt to form a paste.
• Use Japanese rice vinegar, which gives a mild, smooth taste. You can also substitute red wine vinegar, sherry vinegar, cider vinegar, raspberry vinegar or others.
• Use freshly squeezed lime or lemon juice instead of vinegar.
• Instead of extra virgin, use 2 tablespoons mild virgin olive oil and 3 tablespoons nut oil such as walnut, hazelnut or macadamia.

Blue cheese dressing

250 g/9 oz. dolcelatte, Gorgonzola or other blue cheese, crumbled
6 tablespoons extra virgin olive oil
2 tablespoons white wine vinegar
sea salt and freshly ground
black pepper

Makes about 125 ml/½ cup

To make the dressing, put the crumbled cheese in a bowl and crush with a fork. Add 2 tablespoons of the olive oil and mash until creamy, adding the remaining olive oil and the vinegar as you go. If the end result is too thick, beat in a little hot water until the mixture is loose and creamy. Add salt and pepper to taste – take care with the salt, because blue cheese is already quite salty. The dressing will thicken on standing, so you may have beat it again before serving (or you can add a little water or milk to thin it down).

Reduced balsamic vinegar

Reducing an inexpensive balsamic vinegar produces a thick, unctuous dressing and can be used in drops.

300 ml/1 ¼ cups balsamic vinegar

Makes 100 ml/⅓ cup

Put the vinegar in a small saucepan. Bring to the boil, then simmer gently until it is reduced by two-thirds and is the consistency of thick syrup. Let cool, then store in a clean bottle. Use as a salad dressing or a seasoning.

Simple Italian-style dressing

One of the simplest dressings of all is just a drizzle of the very best quality extra virgin olive oil and a squeeze of lemon juice or a mild vinegar. It might be all a simple side salad, such as tomato and red onion, needs. In many Italian restaurants, especially in Italy, you will see a 'cruet' of oil and vinegar or just bottles of vinegar and oil, usually from the local area. You dress your salad to taste. First the salt, then vinegar, then the oil. Simple.

south-east asian dressings

Before the Portuguese took chillies to Asia, pepper and ginger alone satisfied the appetite for hot, spicy tastes. Now you can't think of Asia without chillies! South-east Asian dressings include salt, sour, sweet and hot elements, and cooks add a little more of one or less of another according to taste, traditions and the flavour and texture of what they're dressing. In Vietnam especially, salt components don't appear on the table, so it's up to the cook to decide. The one element diners are trusted to add to taste is chilli. In some Thai restaurants, it's common to be given a 'cruet' set of grated palm sugar, crushed dried chillies, chillies in vinegar and chillies in fish sauce.

Vietnamese chilli-lime dressing

6 tablespoons freshly squeezed lime juice

1 tablespoon Vietnamese fish sauce

2 tablespoons brown sugar

2 fresh red or green chillies, deseeded and very finely chopped

1 garlic clove, crushed

3-cm/1¼-inch piece of fresh ginger, peeled and grated

Makes about 200 ml/¾ cup

Put all the ingredients in a small bowl and beat with a fork until the sugar has dissolved.

Thai fresh chilli dressing

4 tablespoons freshly squeezed lime juice

2 tablespoons Thai fish sauce

2 fresh red or green chillies, deseeded and very finely chopped

Makes about 125 ml/½ cup

Put the lime juice, fish sauce and chillies in a bowl and stir with a spoon until combined.

Spicy Thai dressing

4 tablespoons Thai fish sauce

freshly squeezed juice of 1 lemon or 2 limes

2 teaspoons brown sugar

2 tablespoons red Thai curry paste

Makes about 125 ml/½ cup

Put the fish sauce, lime or lemon juice, sugar and curry paste in a bowl and beat with a fork until combined.

Sesame oil dressing

3-cm/1¼-inch piece of fresh ginger, peeled and sliced

3 spring onions/scallions, chopped

1 fresh red chilli, deseeded and chopped

1 tablespoon Szechuan peppercorns

200 ml/¾ cup peanut oil

4 tablespoons sesame oil

Makes about 375 ml/1½ cups

Put the ginger, spring onions/scallions, chilli and peppercorns in a small blender and pulse to chop. Put the peanut and sesame oils in a saucepan and heat until hot but not smoking. Remove from the heat, add the flavourings, stir, cover with a lid, let cool, then strain.

Lime dressing

1 tablespoon Thai fish sauce

freshly squeezed juice of 1 lime

1 teaspoon brown sugar

Makes about 60 ml/¼ cup

Mix in a small bowl and serve as a dipping sauce, or sprinkled over an Asian-style salad.

Peanut sauce

250 g/2 cups shelled raw peanuts

2 fresh red chillies, deseeded and thinly sliced

2 fresh bird's eye chillies, deseeded and thinly sliced

1 onion, finely chopped

1 garlic clove, crushed

1 teaspoon sea salt

2 teaspoons brown sugar

200 ml/¾ cup tinned coconut milk

Makes about 375 ml/1½ cups

Toast the peanuts in a dry frying pan/skillet set over a low heat. Transfer to a clean, dry kitchen towel, rub off the skins, then put the nuts in a blender. Grind to a coarse meal, then add the chillies, onion, garlic, salt, sugar and coconut milk. Blend to a purée, then transfer to a saucepan and cook over medium heat, stirring, until thickened.

When ready to serve, thin with water to a pourable consistency.

japanese dressings

Japanese salads usually involve just one or two ingredients, simply dressed, served in small quantities, beautifully arranged in small bowls, heaped in a mountain shape. Most common Asian ingredients are now available in larger supermarkets. Japanese ingredients, such as powdered dashi, can be found near the sushi ingredients. Chinese and other Asian markets also sell it in liquid concentrate form.

Sambai-zu

This is a popular everyday Japanese salad dressing, used in many homes. Sweet, salty and sour.

3 tablespoons rice vinegar

1 teaspoon tamari soy sauce

1 tablespoon white sugar

a pinch of sea salt

Makes about 75 ml/⅓ cup

Put all the ingredients in a bowl and beat with a fork until combined.

Kimi-zu

A Japanese version of mayonnaise.

2 egg yolks

½ teaspoon sea salt

1½ tablespoons white sugar

½ teaspoon cornflour/cornstarch

4 tablespoons dashi stock

2 tablespoons rice vinegar

Makes about 200 ml/¾ cup

Put the egg yolks in a heatproof bowl set over a saucepan of simmering water. Don't let the base of the bowl touch the water. Whisk well, then beat in the salt, sugar and cornflour. Gradually stir in the dashi and

vinegar. Continue simmering, stirring until thickened. The cornflour will stop it curdling, but don't let it boil.

Nihai-zu

This is a simple dressing for shellfish and fish salads.

3 tablespoons white rice vinegar

2 tablespoons tamari soy sauce

a pinch of sea salt

Makes about 75 ml/⅓ cup

Put all the ingredients in a bowl and whisk with a fork until combined.

Goma-zu

This sesame seed dressing is good with raw vegetables.

4 tablespoons black sesame seeds

1 tablespoon sugar

2 tablespoons tamari soy sauce

1 tablespoon sake

2 tablespoons rice vinegar

Makes about 200 ml/¾ cup

Toast the sesame seeds in a dry frying pan/skillet set over low heat until aromatic. Using a mortar and pestle, grind to a powder. Add the

sugar and grind again, then stir in the soy sauce, sake and vinegar. If preferred, add 1 tablespoon water or dashi.

Ponzu sauce

This fashionable dressing can be difficult to make because yuzu fruit (a kind of citrus fruit) is rare outside Japan. The juice is sometimes available in specialist stores, or can be ordered.

grated zest and juice of 1 yuzu or small blood orange

tamari soy sauce

Put the grated zest and juice in a bowl, then stir in an equal quantity of soy sauce.

the mayonnaise family

The key to making mayonnaise is to have all the ingredients at room temperature and to add the oil a few drops at a time at first, then more quickly, but not in a continuous stream as many books advise. The emulsion needs time to absorb the oil, so don't overtax it. Don't use all olive oil (unless you're making aïoli) – the flavour is too strong. Use a light oil such as sunflower, but good quality: don't use those labelled 'vegetable oil', because they have usually been heat-extracted (cold-pressed is the healthier option). You can make mayonnaise by hand, or use a food processor if preferred.

Classic mayonnaise

2 egg yolks, at room temperature
1 whole egg (if making in a food processor)
2 teaspoons Dijon mustard
a large pinch of sea salt
2 teaspoons freshly squeezed lemon juice or white wine vinegar
250 ml/1 cup good-quality sunflower, safflower or peanut oil (not corn oil)
125 ml/½ cup virgin olive oil

Makes about 500 ml/2 cups

If making in a food processor, put the egg yolks, whole egg, mustard, salt and lemon juice in the bowl and blend until pale. If making by hand, omit the whole egg. Gradually add the oil, a few drops at a time at first, then more quickly, but in stages, leaving a few seconds between additions to allow the eggs to 'digest' the oil. When all the oil has been added, if the mixture is too thick, add 1 tablespoon warm water. Serve immediately, or press clingfilm/plastic wrap over the surface to prevent a skin from forming. It may be refrigerated for up to 3 days.

Aïoli

An unctuous garlic mayonnaise served with Provençal dishes such as crudités. Crush 4 garlic cloves and put in a food processor at the same time as the eggs. Proceed as in the Classic Mayonnaise recipe, using all olive oil.

Rouille aïoli

Add 1 tablespoon spicy Moroccan harissa paste at the end of the Aïoli recipe to make a quick rouille with a North African accent.

Potato salad dressing

200 ml/¾ cup single/light cream
½ recipe Classic Mayonnaise
1 tablespoon Dijon mustard
2 tablespoons snipped chives

Makes about 375 ml/1½ cups

Stir the cream into the mayonnaise to thin it a little, then stir in the mustard and chives. Alternatively, omit the cream and use a whole recipe of Classic Mayonnaise!

Thousand island dressing

An American classic, great with prawn/shrimp or mild cheese salads.

200 ml/½ recipe Classic Mayonnaise
50 ml/¼ cup low-fat plain yogurt or sour cream
3 tablespoons chilli sauce
½ green bell pepper, finely chopped
½ red bell pepper, roasted and finely chopped (use can use an antipasti-style chargrilled pepper from a jar)
1 teaspoon finely grated onion

Makes about 500 ml/2 cups

Put the mayonnaise and yogurt into a bowl. Add the chilli sauce, peppers and onion and stir well. Serve immediately or cover with clingfilm/plastic wrap and refrigerate for up to 8 hours.

Green goddess dressing

Another great American dressing, traditionally served with a Cobb Salad.

500 ml/1 recipe Classic Mayonnaise
8 canned anchovy fillets, drained and mashed with a fork
2 spring onions/scallions, green and white bits, chopped
a bunch of chives, snipped
a handful of flat-leaf parsley, chopped
2 tablespoons chopped tarragon
4 tablespoons tarragon vinegar

Makes about 750 ml/3 cups

Put all the ingredients in a bowl and stir well. Serve immediately or cover with clingfilm/plastic wrap and refrigerate for up to 8 hours.

Everyone has their favourite classic salad, but all too often they disappoint. Here you'll find authentic recipes that are guaranteed to deliver a delicious forkful every time. As ever, the key to any great salad is using fresh ingredients of the highest quality.

the classics

simple green salad

150 g/6 oz. crisp lettuce, such as cos/romaine or iceberg

100 g/4 oz. soft leaf lettuce, such as butterhead or lamb's lettuce/corn salad

75 g/3 oz. peppery leaves, such as rocket/arugula or watercress OR bitter leaves, such as frisée, with radicchio for added colour

Classic vinaigrette

1 teaspoon Dijon mustard

¼ teaspoon sea salt

⅛ teaspoon freshly ground black pepper

1 tablespoon white wine vinegar

3 tablespoons extra virgin olive oil

Serves 4

Elegant, fresh and vibrant tasting, a classic simple green salad is the perfect accompaniment to any meal.

Wash and thoroughly dry all the salad leaves. Tear any very large leaves into bite-size pieces. To make the classic vinaigrette, whisk together the mustard, salt, pepper and vinegar in a large salad bowl until combined. Whisk in the olive oil. Just before serving, toss the leaves through the dressing. Serve immediately.

Variations
Fresh soft herbs such as basil, tarragon, chervil, mint and chives can be added to give flavour. Match the herb to the meal you are having. For example, tarragon goes very well with chicken; chervil with fish; basil with Mediterranean-style dishes; mint with lamb; and coriander/cilantro with hot spicy foods.

2 thick slices of dense white bread

2 tablespoons olive oil

1 large or 3 baby cos/romaine lettuce

40 g/1 ½ oz. Parmesan, grated or shaved, as preferred

Classic caesar dressing

1 very fresh egg, at room temperature

1 small garlic clove, crushed

1 teaspoon Dijon mustard

1 teaspoon Worcestershire sauce

¼ teaspoon sea salt

⅛ teaspoon freshly ground black pepper

1 tablespoon white wine vinegar

1 tablespoon freshly squeezed lemon juice

4 tablespoons extra virgin olive oil

Serves 4

This recipe is true to the original classic Caesar salad – a rare perfection. Adding any of the variations listed below will turn this into a more substantial meal.

classic caesar salad

Cut the crusts off the bread and discard. Cut the bread into cubes. Heat the olive oil in a frying pan/skillet, add the bread cubes and cook until golden brown. Set aside.

To make the classic Caesar dressing, put the egg in a small saucepan and cover with warm water. Bring to just simmering, turn off the heat and leave the egg for 2 minutes. Run under cold water to stop the egg cooking further. (This recipe uses partially cooked eggs. If you prefer to cook the eggs through, you can do this by increasing the cooking time to 6 minutes. Finely chop the egg before adding it to the dressing.)

Crack the egg into a large serving bowl and whisk in the garlic, mustard, Worcestershire sauce, salt, pepper, vinegar and lemon juice. Slowly whisk in the extra virgin olive oil.

Add the lettuce and toss well, then scatter over the Parmesan cheese and croûtons to serve.

Variations

Chicken Caesar Roast 3–4 chicken breasts until golden and cooked through. Let cool then slice and add to the salad.

Bacon and avocado Caesar Fry 8 rashers/slices of bacon until crisp. Chop and add to the salad with 1 sliced avocado.

Poached egg and anchovy Caesar For a more intense anchovy flavour, you can either add 4 finely chopped anchovy fillets to the dressing or toss whole, mild, good-quality anchovy fillets through the salad. Top each salad with a poached egg to serve.

insalata caprese

The famous Italian *caprese* salad often includes basil. In this recipe, rocket/arugula adds a curious, peppery bite to what is an ancient, well-loved dish. Do use superb, milky, soft *mozzarella di bufala*, the whey-packed cheese made from the rich, very white milk of water buffaloes, not cows. Add ripe, flavourful tomatoes and an exceptional, unfiltered or estate-bottled, first-pressed extra virgin olive oil and this dish becomes sublime. Never refrigerate it: make just a few minutes before eating and serve with some crusty bread and a few herby olives, if liked.

3 buffalo mozzarella cheeses, 150 g/5½ oz. each

4 large, juicy, sun-ripened red tomatoes

4 large handfuls of wild rocket/arugula

6–8 tablespoons unfiltered or estate-bottled, first-pressed extra virgin olive oil, preferably Italian

sea salt and freshly ground black pepper

crusty bread to serve

Serves 4

Drain the mozzarellas. Slice thickly or pull them apart into big rough chunks, showing the grainy strands. Arrange down one side of a large serving platter.

Slice the tomatoes thickly and arrange them in a second line down the middle of the plate. If they are very large, cut them in half first, then into semi-circles. Add the wild rocket/arugula leaves down the other side of the platter.

Sprinkle with salt and pepper, then just before serving trickle the olive oil over the top. Make sure you have crusty bread (slightly char-grilled tastes good) to mop up the juices.

salad niçoise

This French classic is often made with canned tuna, but fresh tuna steaks make it extra special and more filling. You can substitute good-quality bottled tuna if preferred.

8 small waxy potatoes

4 eggs

200 g/7 oz. green beans, trimmed

4 x 160-g/6-oz tuna steaks

2 teaspoons olive oil

150 g/6 oz. crisp lettuce

4 ripe tomatoes, cut into wedges

16 black olives

Simple dressing

2 tablespoons white wine vinegar

1 teaspoon Dijon mustard

4 tablespoons extra virgin olive oil

sea salt and freshly ground black pepper

a ridged griddle pan/skillet

Serves 4

Put the potatoes in a large saucepan of water and bring to the boil then reduce the heat and cook until tender. Drain and halve or quarter if necessary.

Put the eggs in a saucepan and cover with tepid water. Bring to the boil and boil for 4 minutes for medium and 6 minutes for hard-boiled, as preferred. Cool under cold running water, peel and quarter.

Bring a saucepan of water to the boil, add the beans and cook until tender. Drain and refresh with iced water.

Heat a ridged griddle pan/skillet to hot. Rub the tuna with the olive oil and season with salt and pepper. Cook in the pan for 2 minutes on each side, remove from the heat and leave to rest for 5 minutes. Cut into pieces.

Arrange the lettuce, tomatoes, olives, potatoes, egg quarters, beans and tuna on serving plates.

In a bowl, whisk together the vinegar and mustard and season to taste with salt and pepper. Whisk in the extra virgin olive oil until well blended. Pour over each salad just before serving.

1 tablespoon olive oil

4 large chicken breasts with skin on

4 baby gem lettuce, leaves separated

2 avocados, stoned, peeled and cut into 2-cm/¾ in. pieces

½ an iceberg lettuce, cut into chunks

1 large bunch of watercress, stems removed

8 rashers/slices cooked bacon

12 soft-boiled quails' eggs or 3 eggs

200 g/7 oz. baby plum tomatoes, halved

60 g/2¼ oz. firm blue cheese, crumbled

1 recipe Green Goddess Dressing (see page 14)

Serves 4

This American classic was invented in the Roaring Twenties by a Californian restaurateur named Cobb. It's essentially a 'bitser' salad – bitser this and bitser that! It's also a good post-turkey dish, when you have lots of turkey left over and you're looking for an easy way to serve it. Traditionally, the ingredients were arranged in lines but it tastes just as good tumbled together.

cobb salad

Heat the olive oil in a heavy, non-stick pan. Season the chicken and cook for 5–10 minutes on each side over medium/low heat, or until the juices run clear. Take off the heat and let sit for 5 minutes before removing any fat and thinly slicing the meat.

Line a platter with the leaves of the baby gem. Arrange the chicken in a small stack and place the avocado next to it. Compose the other ingredients in piles. Serve with the Green Goddess Dressing.

waldorf salad

3–4 Granny Smith apples

freshly squeezed juice of 1 lemon

2 celery ribs, thinly sliced

125 g/1 cup walnut pieces,
coarsely chopped

125 ml/½ cup Classic Mayonnaise
(see page 14)

Serves 4

This classic salad was first created in in 1890s in the kitchens of the Waldorf Hotel in New York. It is particularly good served as a side with grilled or barbecued meat and suits pork very well, since pork and apples were made for each other. Make it with ripe Granny Smiths so they won't be too tart, or choose crisp red apples instead. Some recipes includes grapes, so if you like them, do add a handful of halved seedless green grapes.

To prepare the salad, cut a few slices of apple with skin for decoration, then peel and core the remainder and cut into matchstick strips, using a mandoline. Toss them in the lemon juice to stop them turning brown.

Finely slice the celery, put it into a salad bowl, add the apples and walnuts, then spoon over the mayonnaise and mix until combined. Spoon into a serving dish, garnish with the reserved apple slices and serve.

Most grains and pulses are mild in flavour and have a pleasing texture so they work well with crunchy vegetables and sharp, citrusy dressings. They add plenty of nutritional content too, often turning a simple salad into a substantial dish.

grains and pulses

warm couscous salad with feta, spring beans and dill

275 g/1¾ cups couscous

400 ml/1¾ cups boiling water

5 tablespoons extra virgin olive oil

1 garlic clove, peeled and crushed

3 shallots, peeled and thinly sliced

2 tablespoons chopped dill

2 tablespoons snipped chives

1 tablespoon finely chopped preserved lemon, or 1 tablespoon zest and flesh of fresh lemon, finely chopped

250 g/8 oz. feta cheese, chopped

150 g/5 oz. sugar snap peas

150 g/5 oz baby broad/fava beans

150 g/5 oz. frozen peas, defrosted

freshly ground black pepper

Serves 4

Dill is quite a floral, grassy herb and a whiff of it conjures up springtime, which is possibly why it is so well complemented by the beans and peas in this dish. Marinating the feta lifts it from a salty, creamy cheese to something much more complex, so it's well worth it, even if it's just for 5 minutes.

Put the couscous in a large bowl and pour over the boiling water. Cover with clingfilm/plastic wrap or a plate and leave to swell for 10 minutes.

Pour the olive oil into a mixing bowl and add the garlic, shallots, dill, chives and preserved lemon and lots of freshly ground black pepper – the coarser the better. Add the feta, turn in the oil and set aside while you cook the beans.

Bring a medium saucepan of unsalted water to the boil. Add the sugar snap peas, bring back to the boil and cook for 1 minute. Add the broad/fava beans, bring back to the boil and cook for 1 minute. Finally, add the peas and cook for 2 minutes. Drain.

Uncover the couscous, stir in the hot beans, transfer to bowls and top with the feta, spooning over the flavoured oil as you go. Stir well before serving.

herb, red onion and quinoa salad with preserved lemon

This refreshing salad is packed with green herbs and has a light touch of spice. It makes the perfect accompaniment to salmon, poultry, pork and lamb.

150 g/1 cup quinoa

1 small red onion

rind of 1 preserved lemon, finely chopped, OR finely grated zest of 1 fresh lemon

75 g/3 oz. rocket/arugula

a large bunch of flat-leaf parsley, stems removed

a small bunch of mint, chopped

a handful of chives, chopped

freshly squeezed juice of 1 lemon

¼ teaspoon ground cinnamon

4 tablespoons extra virgin olive oil

sea salt and freshly ground black pepper

Serves 6

Bring a medium saucepan of salted water to the boil. Rinse the quinoa in a sieve/strainer under cold running water, then add to the boiling water. Cook for 12–15 minutes until tender. Drain and let cool.

Slice the onion very finely, using a mandoline if you have one. Put in a bowl of iced water for 10 minutes. Drain well.

In a bowl, combine the quinoa, onion, preserved lemon rind, rocket/arugula, parsley, mint and chives.

In a small bowl, whisk together the lemon juice, cinnamon and ¼ teaspoon each of salt and pepper. Whisk in the oil.

Toss the salad and dressing together just before serving.

100 g/½ cup wild rice

100 g/½ cup brown basmati rice

100 g/½ cup white long-grain rice

75 g/½ cup currants, soaked
in warm water for 10 minutes,
then drained

75 g/½ cup dried cherries,
chopped if large

1 large bulb of fennel, trimmed and
chopped, feathery tops reserved

1 teaspoon crushed cumin seeds

a bunch of spring onions/scallions,
sliced

50 g/⅓ cup blanched flaked/
slivered almonds, toasted

50 g/⅓ cup shelled and blanched
pistachio nuts, chopped

3 tablespoons chopped
coriander/cilantro

freshly ground black pepper

cos/romaine lettuce leaves,
to serve

Preserved lemon dressing

5 tablespoons extra virgin olive oil

1–2 tablespoons freshly squeezed
lemon juice

1 garlic clove, crushed

2 tablespoons chopped
preserved lemon

1–2 pinches of sugar

Serves 6–8

If you have been put off of rice salad from sampling one too many of the bland variety, this one may well bring you back into the fold. The essential ingredient is preserved lemons, which you can find in gourmet sections in most supermarkets or from an on-line specialist supplier of Moroccan ingredients. This is good with many things, such as fish, chicken, cold roast pork or lamb.

rice salad with preserved lemon dressing

Cook each variety of rice in a separate saucepan of boiling water over medium heat until tender. The wild rice can take up to 40 minutes*, brown rice about 25 minutes and long-grain rice should be tender in 15 minutes. Drain the rice into a colander. Rinse briefly with hot water, then leave to drain well, fluffing up with a fork after 5 minutes.

Meanwhile, make the dressing. Put the oil and the lemon juice in a bowl, whisk well, then whisk in the garlic and preserved lemon. Season to taste with pepper and sugar. Toss the cooked rice with half the dressing, the currants and the cherries.

Heat the remaining oil in a frying pan/skillet and cook the fennel and crushed cumin seeds gently for 5 minutes until softened but not browned. Add the onions and cook for another 1–2 minutes. Stir into the rice with the nuts, coriander/cilantro and fennel tops, chopped. Let the salad stand for 30 minutes, then stir in the remaining dressing and serve with the lettuce leaves.

*Note To cut down the cooking time for wild rice, soak it for 30 minutes in cold water before cooking.

½ teaspoon sea salt

200 g/1 cup brown rice

140 g/1 cup hazelnuts

4 spring onions/scallions, thinly sliced

leaves from a large bunch of mint

leaves from a large bunch of basil (Thai basil if available)

leaves from a large bunch of coriander/cilantro

2 teaspoons sesame oil

edible flower petals (optional)

Kaffir lime dressing

1 tablespoon sugar, preferably palm, chopped

2 tablespoons rice vinegar

1 tablespoon Japanese or golden soy sauce

1 tablespoon freshly squeezed lime juice

1 tablespoon Thai fish sauce

2 kaffir lime leaves, tough stems removed, very finely shredded

Serves 6

brown rice, hazelnut and herb salad with kaffir lime dressing

This deliciously nutty salad has a hint of South-east Asian flavour. Great served with fish and shellfish, it's also good with meats that have been cooked on the barbecue, especially ones that have been marinated in soy sauce.

To make the kaffir lime dressing, gently heat the sugar and vinegar together in a small saucepan, stirring until the sugar has dissolved. Let cool, then combine with the soy sauce, lime juice, fish sauce and kaffir lime leaves. Set aside until needed.

Bring 500 ml/2 cups water to the boil, add the salt and rice and bring back to the boil. Stir, cover, lower the heat to very low and cook undisturbed for 25 minutes. Turn off the heat, let rest for 5 minutes, then stir with a fork to fluff up (drain off excess water if necessary). Put in a serving bowl, toss with the dressing and leave to cool.

Preheat the oven to 170°C (325°F) Gas 3.

Spread the hazelnuts out on a baking sheet. Toast in the preheated oven for 12 minutes, stirring once. Put the nuts in a clean kitchen towel and rub vigorously until the skins come loose. Shake or blow the loosened skins away, and continue rubbing the nuts until they are mostly free from skins. Roughly chop. Toss the rice with the hazelnuts, spring onions/scallions, mint, basil, coriander/cilantro and oil. Scatter with petals, if using, to serve.

250 g/1¼ cups Asian black rice or wild rice

Asian dressing

2 stalks of lemongrass, outer leaves discarded, remainder very finely chopped

3-cm/1-inch piece of fresh ginger, peeled, grated and juice squeezed

1 fresh green chilli, halved, deseeded and finely chopped

freshly squeezed juice of 1 lime

125 ml/½ cup fish sauce

2 tablespoons brown sugar

Chilli greens

a handful of asparagus, halved

a handful of sugar snap peas

a handful of green beans, halved

100 g/1 cup broad/fava beans, boiled and skinned (optional)

1 fresh red chilli, deseeded and chopped

4 spring onions/scallions, sliced diagonally

Serves 4

black rice salad with chilli greens

If you can't find black rice, use wild rice here. This deliciously different recipe is Asian in influence. For a variation simply change the dressing to a classic vinaigrette, use red onion instead of spring onion/scallion and omit the chilli.

Put the dressing ingredients into a saucepan, bring to the boil and simmer until the sugar has dissolved. Taste and add water if necessary. Let cool.

Put the rice into a saucepan, cover with water to one finger's joint above the top of the rice and bring to the boil. Cover tightly with a lid, reduce the heat and simmer for 14 minutes (12 for white rice). Turn off the heat, do NOT remove the lid, and set aside for 12 minutes. Remove the lid. The rice should be perfectly fluffy. If not (and this sometimes happens with black rice), put the lid back on and boil hard for about 1 minute. Remove from the heat, drain, then run it under cold water. Drain again and transfer to a bowl.

Put the asparagus stalk ends into a saucepan of boiling salted water for 1½ minutes or until you can just pierce them with a fork. Scoop out and drain in a colander under cold running water. Add the tips and sugar snaps and cook as before for about 30 seconds, until just tender. Drain under cold running water. Cook the green beans and broad/fava beans, if using, in the same way. Put all the greens in a bowl, add the chilli and spring onions/scallions and mix well.

Add the chilli greens to the rice and sprinkle with the dressing. Stir gently, then serve.

This hearty version of the traditional and much-loved summer salad incorporates satisfyingly chewy barley. If you are able to buy good-quality dried Greek oregano from speciality food stores, it will make all the difference to the flavour.

greek barley salad

100 g/⅔ cup pearl barley

freshly squeezed juice and finely grated zest of 1 lemon

2 teaspoons white wine or red wine vinegar

4 tablespoons extra virgin olive oil

1 red onion, thinly sliced

4 tomatoes, chopped

1 large cucumber or 2 small (Lebanese), deseeded and chopped

1 green pepper, deseeded and chopped

20 kalamata olives

150 g/5–6 oz. feta cheese

1 teaspoon dried oregano

sea salt and freshly ground black pepper

Serves 4

Cook the barley in a saucepan of boiling salted water for 30 minutes or until tender. Drain and set aside until needed.

In a large serving bowl, whisk together the lemon juice and zest, vinegar and oil, then stir in the warm barley and mix well. Leave to cool.

Soak the onion in a bowl of iced water for 10 minutes (this will crisp it up and soften the flavour). Drain well.

Add the drained onion to the barley along with the tomatoes, cucumber, green pepper and olives and mix to combine. Season to taste with salt and pepper.

Crumble the feta over the top of the salad and sprinkle with oregano. Serve immediately.

apple and wheat salad with cider mayonnaise

90 g/1 cup bulghur wheat

2 spring onions/scallions, finely chopped

1 celery rib, finely chopped

1 red (bell) pepper, deseeded and finely chopped

1 green apple, cored and finely chopped

Cider mayonnaise

1 tablespoon grainy mustard

1 tablespoon runny honey

2 tablespoons cider vinegar

2 tablespoons mayonnaise

a large bunch of flat-leaf parsley, stems removed

freshly ground black pepper

Serves 4–6

Bulghur wheat-based salads such as tabbouleh are quick, easy and substantial. You could also substitute another grain, such as barley, cooked according to the packet instructions.

Put the bulghur wheat in a bowl and cover with cold water. Leave to soak for 30 minutes until tender but not too soft. Drain well and press down hard on the bulghur wheat with the back of a spoon to squeeze out excess water.

Put the bulghur wheat in a salad bowl with the spring onions/scallions, celery, red pepper and apple.

To make the cider mayonnaise, whisk together the mustard, apple syrup, vinegar and mayonnaise in a small bowl and add black pepper to taste. Add this to the bulghur mixture, cover and refrigerate until needed.

Remove the salad from the refrigerator about 30 minutes before serving and bring to room temperature. Stir in the chopped parsley to serve.

420-g/14-oz. can white beans (butter or cannellini), drained and rinsed

420-g/14-oz. can borlotti beans, drained and rinsed

300 g/10 oz. green beans, trimmed

75 g/½ cup small fresh or frozen broad/fava beans

120 g/1 cup beansprouts

Lemon and poppy seed dressing

3 tablespoons poppy seeds

1 small red onion

1 tablespoon runny honey

1 teaspoon finely grated lemon zest

1 teaspoon sea salt flakes

¼ teaspoon freshly ground black pepper

2 tablespoons freshly squeezed lemon juice

4 tablespoons olive oil (lemon-infused if available)

Serves 6

five-bean salad with lemon and poppy seed dressing

This is a more dramatic take on the old-style bean salad and is the perfect foil to rich meats such as sausages. The lemon and poppy seed dressing works well with any green salad or potato salad and is delicious drizzled over grilled vegetables.

To make the lemon and poppy seed dressing, heat a frying pan/skillet over medium heat and add the poppy seeds. Cook, tossing in the pan, for 3 minutes until toasted. Let cool.

Grate the onion and put in a bowl with the toasted poppy seeds, honey, lemon zest, salt and pepper. Whisk in the lemon juice and then the oil.

In a large bowl, combine the drained cannellini and borlotti beans. Pour over the lemon and poppy seed dressing and toss well. Set aside while you prepare the other beans.

Bring a saucepan of water to the boil. Add the green beans and boil for 5 minutes until just tender. Drain and refresh in plenty of iced water.

Bring another saucepan of water to the boil. Add the broad/fava beans and boil for 2 minutes until just blanched. Drain and refresh in plenty of iced water. If using frozen beans, peel off the tough outer layer and discard.

Pour boiling water over the beansprouts to blanch, then refresh in plenty of iced water.

Drain the green beans, broad/fava beans and beansprouts well. Add to the dressed beans and toss well before serving.

1 kg/2 cups cooked or canned chickpeas, rinsed and drained

4 marinated artichoke hearts

4 large sun-blushed tomatoes

250 g/8 oz. very ripe cherry tomatoes, halved

8 spring onions/scallions, sliced diagonally

a handful of basil leaves, torn

a small bunch of chives, snipped

leaves from 4 sprigs of flat-leaf parsley, chopped

50 g/2 oz. fresh Parmesan, shaved

1 tablespoon cracked black pepper

Dijon dressing

6 tablespoons extra virgin olive oil

1 tablespoon freshly squeezed lemon juice or sherry vinegar

1 teaspoon Dijon mustard

1 small garlic clove, crushed

sea salt and freshly ground black pepper

Serves 4

Chickpeas, like all dried pulses, drink up flavours, but unlike some, chickpeas can be relied upon not to fall apart. That means they are great for packed lunches, picnics and other make-ahead occasions. You can part-prepare them, so that the dressing soaks into the chickpeas, then add the fresh ingredients just before serving.

quick chickpea salad

Put the dressing ingredients in a bowl and beat with a fork. Add the chickpeas, artichoke hearts and sun-blushed tomatoes, if using, and toss in the dressing. Cover with a plate and chill for up to 4 hours.

When ready to serve, add the cherry tomatoes, spring onions/scallions, basil, chives and parsley. Stir gently, then sprinkle with the Parmesan and pepper. Serve immediately.

puy lentil salad

This is a super quick supper recipe that uses ready-cooked tiny black Puy lentils. You can now buy these pre-cooked and seasoned in a vacuum package so hold back on the salt if this is what you are using.

400 g/2 cups cooked Puy lentils (either canned or vacuum packed)

4 preserved baby artichokes, either char-grilled in oil or canned, quartered

1 red onion, halved lengthways and finely sliced

50 g/¼ cup black kalamata olives, drained of oil

150 g/6 oz. feta cheese, cut into cubes or crumbled into big pieces

a handful of flat-leaf parsley leaves, coarsely chopped

Dressing

1 tablespoon cider vinegar

3–4 tablespoons extra virgin olive oil

a pinch of sea salt (taste the lentils first as they may already be seasoned)

freshly ground black pepper

Serves 4

Put the cooked lentils in a large bowl, then add the vinegar, oil, salt (if using) and black pepper.

Add the artichokes, onion, feta cheese and herbs, then toss gently to combine. Add a little more salt and pepper to taste, then serve, sprinkled with herbs.

Variation

For an Italian feel, replace the feta with bocconcini or buffalo mozzarella cheese, torn into long shreds, add halved cherry plum tomatoes and replace the parsley with fresh basil. Add a sprinkle of balsamic vinegar before serving.

2 cobs/ears of sweetcorn (corn), husked

4 large, ripe tomatoes, cut into wedges

400-g/14-oz. jar or can artichoke hearts, drained

1 tablespoon white wine vinegar

3 tablespoons olive or avocado oil

leaves from a large bunch of basil

sea salt flakes and freshly ground black pepper

Polenta-crumbed aubergine

2 small aubergines/eggplant

1 egg

1 tablespoon milk

90 g/⅔ cup instant polenta or fine cornmeal

1 teaspoon cumin seeds, lightly crushed

2 tablespoons chopped fresh thyme or ½ teaspoon dried

30 g/¼ cup plain/all-purpose flour

½ teaspoon sea salt

2 tablespoons olive or avocado oil

Serves 4

summer vegetables with polenta-crumbed aubergine

Sweetcorn and tomatoes are seasonal vegetables that really are much better in the summertime. Dress them very simply so their flavour shines through. Polenta makes a terrific instant crumb for vegetables, adding crunch and a subtle corn flavour.

Bring a large saucepan of water to the boil and add the sweetcorn. Cook for 8 minutes or until tender when pierced with a knife. Drain and set aside to cool.

Cut the kernels off the cobs/ears, trying to keep the corn kernels in large pieces. Arrange the corn on a plate with the tomatoes and artichoke hearts. Drizzle over the vinegar and oil and season to taste with salt and pepper.

To make the polenta-crumbed aubergine/eggplant, slice the aubergines into slices 1 cm/½ inch thick. Beat the egg together with the milk and put in a shallow dish. In a separate dish, combine the polenta, cumin and thyme. Put the flour and salt in a third dish.

Heat the oil in a large frying pan/skillet set over medium heat. Dip each slice of aubergine/eggplant first in the flour, then the egg and milk mixture and finally into the polenta. Fry for 3 minutes on each side until golden and cooked through. Arrange the polenta-crumbed aubergine/eggplant on top of the prepared vegetables and garnish with the basil leaves. Serve immediately.

A substantial salad with a protein element in the form of meat, poultry or fish makes a satisfying meal, and often one that is quick and easy to prepare. An added plus is that the inclusion of fresh vegetables and fruit creates a colourful and appealing plate.

meat, poultry and fish

1 tablespoon Sichuan peppercorns

2 garlic cloves, chopped

1 teaspoon sea salt

2 teaspoons groundnut oil

400-g/14-oz. piece of beef fillet

2 tablespoons rice vinegar (black)

2 tablespoons Japanese or golden soy sauce

2 teaspoons sesame oil

2 teaspoons sugar

½ teaspoon red dried chilli/hot pepper flakes

4 yellow bell peppers, cut into 3 lengthways and deseeded

500 g/1lb. fresh asparagus, trimmed and cut into 3-cm/1½-inch pieces

250 g/9 oz. frozen edamame/soy beans

60 g/1 cup beansprouts

Sweet soy dressing

1 tablespoon Japanese or golden soy sauce

1 tablespoon freshly squeezed lemon juice

1 tablespoon rice vinegar

1 tablespoon sugar

½ teaspoon crushed fresh red chilli

Serves 4

twice-marinated beef salad

This salad uses very rare lean beef fillet; if you want to cook it through, cook in an oven preheated to 180°C (350°F) Gas 4 for 15 minutes before placing in the second marinade.

Put the Sichuan peppercorns, garlic and salt in a mortar and grind to a paste, adding the groundnut oil gradually until incorporated. Rub this all over the beef and leave for 5 minutes to marinate. In a medium-sized non-reactive bowl, mix together the vinegar, soy sauce, sesame oil, sugar and chilli/hot pepper flakes.

Heat a griddle pan/skillet to very hot, add the beef and sear on each side for 1 minute until browned all over. Remove from the heat and immediately put in the marinade, turning to coat well. Let cool, cover and refrigerate for at least 1 hour, but preferably overnight, turning occasionally.

Cook the peppers skin-side up under a preheated grill/broiler for about 10 minutes until blackened and soft. Put in a bowl, cover with clingfilm/plastic wrap and leave for 10 minutes. Peel off all the blackened skin and cut the flesh into strips. Put on serving plates. Cook the asparagus in boiling water for 3 minutes until tender, then quickly refresh with iced water and drain well. Add to the peppers. Cook the edamame beans in boiling water for 3 minutes, then quickly refresh with iced water. Remove the beans from the pods and add to the peppers and asparagus. Put the beansprouts in a sieve/strainer and pour over boiling water to blanch, then quickly refresh with iced water and drain well. Add to the peppers, asparagus and edamame beans.

To make the sweet soy dressing, combine the soy sauce, lemon juice, vinegar, sugar and fresh chilli in a small bowl. Stir until the sugar has dissolved. Just before serving, slice the beef as thinly as possible and add to the salad, pour over the dressing and toss. Serve immediately.

4 bundles of beanthread vermicelli noodles, about 30 g/1 oz. each (optional)

2 tablespoons dark soy sauce

1 tablespoon fish sauce

1 tablespoon brown sugar

500 g/1 lb. beef fillet/tenderloin

4 small pink Thai shallots, or 2 regular, thinly sliced

1 Mini cucumber or 10 cm/4-inch piece of regular cucumber, thinly sliced

1 stalk of lemongrass, outer leaves removed and discarded, remainder very thinly sliced

Dressing

4 tablespoons freshly squeezed lime juice

4 tablespoons fish sauce

1 teaspoon brown sugar (palm if available)

To serve

1 ripe mango, peeled and cut into 1-cm/½-inch cubes

2 fresh red chillies, finely sliced diagonally

2 spring onions/scallions, thinly sliced

a large handful of mint leaves

Serves 4

The beef in this recipe is char-grilled but very rare. If you don't like rare meat, substitute something else, don't cook the meat until it's well done or even medium. You could try crispy roasted duck legs, poached chicken or prawns/shrimp. The mango isn't traditional, but its juicy sweetness contrasts well with the fiery chillies. Papaya is also good.

thai mango beef salad

If serving with noodles, put them in a bowl and cover with hot water. Let soak for about 15 minutes, then drain. Keep in a bowl of cold water until ready to serve, then drain and cut into short lengths, about 5–10 cm/2–4 inches, with kitchen shears.

Put the soy sauce, fish sauce and sugar into a bowl and beat with a fork to dissolve the sugar. Add the beef and turn to coat. Set aside for 1–2 hours to develop the flavours. When ready to cook, preheat a outdoor grill or stove-top grill pan until very hot. Put the meat on the grill or in the pan and cook slowly, turning from time to time, until the surface is well browned and the middle still pink, about 5 minutes in total, depending on the thickness of the meat. Remove from the heat and set aside in a warm place for about 5 minutes to set the juices. Put the meat on a board and slice thinly crossways. Cut the slices into bite-size strips about 5 cm/2 inches long.

Mix the dressing ingredients in a large bowl, beating with a fork to dissolve the sugar. Add the beef slices and any meat juices, the shallots, cucumber and lemongrass. Toss well.

Put a pile of noodles, if using, into each serving bowl, then add the dressed salad. Add the mango, chillies and spring onions/scallions, then spoon any remaining dressing from the bowl over each serving. Top with mint leaves and serve immediately.

lemon-rubbed lamb and orzo salad

This colourful salad can be made well ahead of time; just cook and add the lamb before serving. It's full of the flavours of summer.

3 garlic cloves, crushed

finely grated zest of 2 lemons and freshly squeezed juice of 1

3 tablespoons olive oil

300-g/10-oz. piece of lean lamb fillet

1 large red bell pepper

1 large yellow bell pepper

250 g/1⅓ cups orzo (rice-shaped pasta)

20 cherry tomatoes

400-g/14-oz. can or jar of preserved artichoke hearts, drained and quartered

a small red onion, thinly sliced

4 tablespoons fresh green pesto

4 tablespoons pine nuts, toasted

leaves from a small bunch of basil

sea salt and freshly ground black pepper

Serves 4

Preheat the oven to 220°C (425°F) Gas 7.

In a small bowl, combine the garlic and lemon zest with 1 tablespoon of the oil and season with salt and pepper. Rub this over the lamb and set aside until needed.

Preheat the grill/broiler to hot. Put the lamb under the grill and cook for 2 minutes each side, then transfer to a roasting pan and cook in the preheated oven for 5 minutes for medium rare or up to 10 minutes for more well done. Remove from the oven, wrap in foil and leave to rest for 10 minutes.

Cut the peppers into thick strips, discarding the stems and seeds. Cook under the hot grill/broiler until tender. Set aside.

Cook the orzo according to the packet instructions. Drain and toss with the remaining 2 tablespoons oil, lemon juice, peppers, cherry tomatoes, artichokes, onion and pesto.

Place the salad on serving plates. Slice the lamb and arrange it on top. Scatter with the pine nuts and basil leaves to serve.

pork and lentil salad

200 g/1 cup Puy or French green lentils

1 teaspoon Dijon mustard

2 tablespoons balsamic vinegar

½ teaspoon sea salt

½ teaspoon freshly ground black pepper

4 tablespoons extra virgin olive oil

250 g/8 oz. button mushrooms

1 tablespoon olive oil

finely grated zest of 1 lemon

2 garlic cloves, crushed

2 tablespoons rosemary needles, chopped

350-g/12-oz. piece of pork eye fillet/tenderloin

100 ml/scant ½ cup red wine

100 g/4 oz. baby spinach leaves, washed

16 cherry tomatoes, halved

Serves 4

This is a hearty and delicious salad. The Puy lentils give a lovely nutty texture and a rustic feel to the dish.

Put the lentils in a saucepan with plenty of cold water. Bring to the boil, then reduce to a simmer and cook for 20 minutes. Drain and set aside.

In a large bowl, whisk together the Dijon mustard, vinegar and ¼ teaspoon each of the salt and pepper, then whisk in the extra virgin olive oil. Add the mushrooms and warm lentils and toss well to coat. Set aside to marinate.

In a small bowl, mix together the olive oil, lemon zest, garlic, rosemary and remaining ¼ teaspoon each of the salt and pepper. Rub this mixture all over the pork fillets.

Heat a frying pan/skillet to medium, add the pork and cook for 5 minutes on each side. Remove the pork from the pan to a chopping board and leave to rest for 5 minutes, then slice thinly.

Pour the wine into the hot frying pan/skillet and let it bubble, stirring in any marinade left in the pan. Pour this over the lentils and mushrooms.

Add the sliced pork to the lentils and mushrooms along with the spinach leaves and cherry tomatoes and toss to combine. Serve immediately.

chicken, courgette and bulghur salad with pomegranate vinaigrette

2 garlic cloves, crushed

finely grated zest of 1 lemon

1 teaspoon allspice berries, crushed

2 tablespoons thyme leaves

½ teaspoon sea salt flakes

½ teaspoon freshly ground black pepper

3 tablespoons olive oil

4 skin-on chicken breasts or leg and thigh pieces

6 courgettes/zucchini

100 g/⅔ cup bulghur wheat

leaves from a small bunch of flat-leaf parsley

4 tablespoons pomegranate seeds (optional)

Pomegranate vinaigrette

1 tablespoon white wine vinegar

2 tablespoons pomegranate molasses

3 tablespoons extra virgin olive oil

Serves 4

Serve this exotic salad with plenty of warmed Middle Eastern-style flatbreads on the side.

Preheat the oven to 180°C (350°F) Gas 4.

In a small bowl, mix together the garlic, lemon zest, allspice, thyme, ¼ teaspoon each of the salt and pepper and 2 tablespoons of the olive oil. Put the chicken pieces in a dish and loosen the skin by sliding your hand between the skin and flesh. Rub the oil mixture under the skin. Roast in the preheated oven for 30 minutes for breasts and 50 minutes for leg and thigh pieces. Let cool, then slice or tear the meat into pieces.

Cut the courgettes/zucchini in half, then slice each half into quarters lengthways. Toss in a bowl with the remaining tablespoon of olive oil and ¼ teaspoon each of the salt and pepper. Place in a roasting pan and roast for 20 minutes.

Put the bulghur wheat in a bowl and cover with cold water. Leave to soak for 30 minutes until tender but not too soft. Drain well and press down hard on the wheat with the back of a large spoon to squeeze out any excess water.

To make the vinaigrette, whisk together the vinegar and pomegranate molasses in a small bowl, then whisk in the extra virgin olive oil.

Arrange the bulghur wheat, chicken, courgettes/zucchini and parsley on a serving dish and pour over the dressing. Toss lightly, then scatter over the pomegranate seeds, if using.

Larb is eaten all over Thailand and Laos. It's usually served with sticky rice and scooped up with the fingers. The trick is to get the balance right between the salty fish sauce, sour-sweet lime and heat from the cayenne. The ground rice may seem a little unusual but it adds a good crunch and a distinctive flavour. Chopped, dry roasted peanuts can be substituted.

thai chicken larb

1 tablespoon white rice

2 celery ribs, thinly sliced

1 red onion, thinly sliced

500 g/1 lb. cooked chicken, shredded

2 tablespoons chopped mint leaves

25 g/¼ cup coriander/cilantro leaves

250 g/8 oz. cherry tomatoes, quartered

¼ teaspoon cayenne pepper

8 Boston lettuce leaves

sticky rice, to serve (optional)

Dressing

5 tablespoons freshly squeezed lime juice

3 tablespoons Thai fish sauce

3 tablespoons palm sugar or demerara sugar

1 garlic clove, peeled and crushed

a clean coffee mill

Serves 4

Put the rice in a frying pan/skillet and toast until golden. Grind in a coffee mill until very fine.

To make the dressing, combine the lime juice, fish sauce, a touch of palm sugar and the garlic, then taste. Add more of the sugar if you prefer it sweeter.

Mix the celery, onion and chicken in a bowl and pour over the dressing. Just before serving, stir in the mint, coriander/cilantro, tomatoes and cayenne pepper, to taste. Transfer to serving bowls lined with the lettuce leaves and serve with sticky rice, if desired.

marinated chicken, raisin and chilli salad with hazelnut dressing

a 2-kg/4-lb. chicken

1.5 litres/6 cups good chicken or vegetable stock

a handful of raisins

100 g/1 cup blanched hazelnuts, toasted until dark golden

1 teaspoon dried chilli/hot pepper flakes, or to taste

leaves from a small bunch of flat-leaf parsley, chopped

sea salt and freshly ground black pepper

Hazelnut dressing

6 tablespoons hazelnut oil

2 tablespoons red wine vinegar

1 tablespoon caster sugar

Serves 4–6

Everyone seems to love this moist marinated chicken salad. For the best flavour, be sure to toast the hazelnuts until dark golden. If time is short, you could cheat a little and buy a freshly cooked spit-roasted chicken.

Put the chicken in a very large saucepan and cover with the stock. Bring to the boil. Turn down the heat and poach the chicken for about 1 hour, or until the juices run clear when the chicken is tested with a skewer at the thickest part of the leg. Leave to cool in the stock, then transfer to a chopping board. Using a rolling pin, give the chicken a few good thwacks along the breast. This will make it much easier to shred. Shred the meat into a large bowl. Add the raisins, hazelnuts and chilli flakes.

To make the hazelnut dressing, stir the hazelnut oil, vinegar and sugar together and season to taste. Add to the chicken along with the parsley, toss well and leave to marinate in a cool place (not the fridge) for at least 1 hour. Serve at room temperature.

bang-bang chicken salad

Salad

a 2.5-kg/5-lb. free-range chicken

1.5 litres/6 cups chicken or vegetable stock

3 carrots, peeled and shredded

1 small cabbage, peeled and shredded

3 mixed bell peppers, cut into strips and deseeded

100 g/1 cup sugar snap peas, halved diagonally

3 tablespoons toasted sesame oil

50 g/scant ¼ cup sesame seeds

Sauce

200 g/½ cup peanut butter

3–4 tablespoons shop-bought sweet chilli sauce

2-cm/1-inch piece of fresh ginger, peeled and grated

3 tablespoons toasted sesame oil

2 tablespoons extra virgin olive oil

Serves 4

This is just as the title says – a bit like bang-bang chicken! To save time, you could cheat and use a bought, ready-roasted chicken or even smoked chicken breasts. You can substitute ready-cooked duck from a Chinese restaurant, too.

Put the chicken in a large saucepan and cover with the stock. Bring to the boil. Turn down the heat and poach the chicken for about 1 hour, or until the juices run clear when the chicken is tested with a skewer at the thickest part of the leg. Leave to cool in the stock, then transfer to a chopping board. Using a rolling pin, give the chicken a few good thwacks along the breast. This will make it much easier to shred. Shred the meat into a large bowl.

Mix together the carrots, cabbage, peppers and sugar snap peas in the serving bowls. Top with the shredded chicken.

Heat the sesame oil in a small frying pan/skillet and fry the sesame seeds until golden.

To make the sauce, put the peanut butter, chilli sauce, ginger, sesame oil and olive oil in a saucepan, whisk to combine and heat gently over low heat.

Drizzle some of the sauce over the chicken and scatter with the sesame seeds. Serve immediately, with the remaining sauce alongside.

A delicious festive salad. The frisée adds a slight bitterness that works well, but you can substitute any other type of salad leaf – baby spinach works well.

duck, sausage, sweet potato and cherry salad

4 duck legs

3 tablespoons olive oil

½ teaspoon ground cinnamon

3 sweet potatoes (about 200 g/ 7 oz. each), peeled

1 teaspoon sea salt flakes

8 thin sausages, duck or pork

1 tablespoon sherry vinegar or cider vinegar

finely grated zest of 1 orange and 2 tablespoons freshly squeezed juice

1 tablespoon runny honey

1 teaspoon Dijon mustard

4 tablespoons extra virgin olive oil

1 frisée lettuce, leaves separated

24 fresh dark red cherries, halved and pitted

Serves 4

Preheat the oven to 180°C (350°F) Gas 4.

Slash the duck legs a few times through the flesh. Put 2 tablespoons of the olive oil in a small bowl and whisk in the cinnamon. Use your fingers to rub the oil into the duck. Put the duck in a roasting pan and roast in the preheated oven for 1 hour, turning occasionally.

Cut the sweet potatoes into cubes and toss in a bowl with the remaining olive oil and ½ teaspoon of the salt flakes.

Remove the duck from the roasting pan and set aside to cool. Pour most of the rendered fat off the roasting pan and discard (or reserve for roasting potatoes another time). Add the sausages and sweet potatoes to the roasting pan and coat with the little fat left from the duck. Roast for 30 minutes, stirring twice. Remove from the oven and let cool. Cut the sausages into quarters. Slice the meat from the duck legs.

In a bowl, whisk together the vinegar, orange zest and juice, honey, mustard and remaining ½ teaspoon salt flakes. Slowly whisk in the extra virgin olive oil until incorporated.

Arrange the frisée on serving plates. Top with the duck, sausages, sweet potatoes and cherries. Pour over the dressing and serve immediately.

vietnamese duck salad with table salad herbs

2 duck legs

4 handfuls of beansprouts, rinsed and drained

1 young carrot

6 spring onions/scallions, halved, then finely sliced lengthways

a handful of mint leaves (Vietnamese mint if available)

a handful of Asian basil leaves (optional)

1 recipe Vietnamese Chilli-lime Dressing (see page 10)

2 tablespoons dry roasted peanuts, finely chopped

sea salt and freshly ground black pepper

Serves 4

This recipe is based on a traditional chicken and peanut salad, made with stir-fried chicken mince. Butchers often sell pairs of duck legs quite cheaply as everyone wants the breasts. If you rub them with a little salt and pepper, then roast them until the skin is crispy, they are perfect for this Asian-style salad.

Preheat the oven to 200°C (400°F) Gas 6.

Rub the duck legs with salt and pepper and roast in the preheated oven for about 45 minutes–1 hour, until the skin is crisp and the meat tender.

When cooked, remove and set aside until cool enough to handle. Pull the meat and crispy skin off the bones and discard the bones or keep them for stock. Try to use freshly cooked duck for salads, but if you must refrigerate it, reheat it before using. (Most meats, but especially fatty ones, are nicer if warm or cool, not cold.)

To trim the beansprouts, pinch off the tails and remove the bean from between the little leaves (optional).

To prepare the carrot, peel and shred into long matchsticks on a mandoline or the large blade of a box grater.

Pile the beansprouts on to serving plates. Add the carrot and duck and top with the spring onions/scallions, mint and basil leaves, if using. Drizzle over the dressing, toss to coat and top with the toasted peanuts, then serve.

pickled salmon with fennel and cucumber salad

500-g/1-lb. salmon fillet, skinned and boned

3–4 shallots, thinly sliced

4 tablespoons chopped dill

1 fennel bulb, with fronds if possible

½ cucumber, halved lengthways and deseeded

freshly squeezed juice of 1 lemon

1 teaspoon wholegrain mustard

3 tablespoons olive oil, plus extra for drizzling (optional)

sea salt and freshly ground black pepper

Pickling liquid

200 ml/scant 1 cup white or rice vinegar

2 teaspoons sea salt

4 tablespoons sugar

finely grated zest of 1 lemon

Serve this salad with new potatoes to make the perfect light meal for a warm evening. The fish is marinated for several days, so do prepare ahead.

To make the pickling liquid, combine the vinegar, 100 ml/½ cup water, salt, sugar and lemon zest in a saucepan and bring to the boil. Simmer for 3 minutes, then let cool.

Put the salmon fillet in a shallow, non-reactive container with the shallots and dill. Pour over the pickling liquid and cover tightly. Leave in the refrigerator for 2–3 days, turning the salmon once a day.

To assemble the salad, remove the salmon from the pickling liquid and slice it into thin strips. Arrange the salmon on serving plates with a few of the pickled shallots.

Slice the fennel and cucumber very thinly, using a mandoline if you have one, and put in a bowl. Chop the green fennel fronds, if available, very finely and add 3 tablespoonfuls to the bowl.

In a small bowl, whisk together the lemon juice, mustard and oil and season to taste with salt and pepper. Just before serving, toss the dressing through the fennel and cucumber salad and arrange a little on top of the salmon. Drizzle with extra oil to serve, if liked.

This uncomplicated salad is best served with fresh bread to makes a filling meal. As it features two canned ingredients it can usually be whipped up at short notice. If you have tuna in good-quality olive oil, make use of the oil in the salad.

tuna and cannellini bean salad

1 red onion, thinly sliced

185-g/6-oz can or jar of tuna in olive oil, drained

410-g/14-oz can cannellini beans, drained and rinsed

a large bunch of flat-leaf parsley, chopped

freshly squeezed juice of 1 lemon

4 tablespoons extra virgin olive oil (or oil from the tuna if good quality)

sea salt and freshly ground black pepper

fresh bread, to serve

Serves 2–3

Soak the onion slices in iced water for 10 minutes. Drain well.

Put the onion, tuna, cannellini beans and parsley in a large mixing bowl. Add the lemon juice and oil (from the can or jar if good quality) and toss gently to combine.

Season to taste with salt and plenty of black pepper. Spoon onto serving plates and serve with plenty of fresh crusty bread.

smoked mackerel and bulghur wheat salad

The creamy horseradish dressing is a fabulous complement to the richness of the smoked mackerel, while the raw vegetables add crunch and colour.

60 g/½ cup bulghur wheat

1 tablespoon freshly squeezed lemon juice

1 tablespoon snipped chives

½ yellow bell pepper, deseeded and diced

8 radishes, sliced

75 g/3 oz. baby spinach leaves, rinsed

150 g/5–6 oz. smoked mackerel fillets, flaked from the skin and checked for small bones

Dressing

3 tablespoons fromage frais or sour cream

2 teaspoons horseradish sauce

1 teaspoon snipped chives

freshly ground black pepper

Serves 2

Cook the bulghur wheat in a saucepan of lightly salted boiling water for 15 minutes or until tender. Drain, then mix with the lemon juice, chives, yellow pepper and radishes.

Divide the spinach leaves between serving bowls, spoon the bulghur wheat on top, then add the flaked smoked mackerel.

Mix the dressing ingredients together and drizzle over the fish. and serve immediately.

ceviche

750 g/1½ lbs. very fresh skinless white fish fillets

1 red onion, halved and thinly sliced

1 red or green fresh chilli, deseeded and finely chopped

1 teaspoon grated fresh ginger

freshly squeezed juice of 6 limes

½–1 teaspoon caster sugar, plus extra to taste

½ teaspoon coriander seeds, toasted and ground

5 tablespoons mild olive oil

finely grated zest of 1 small lime

2 ripe avocados, peeled, pitted and sliced

1 ripe but firm papaya (pawpaw), peeled, deseeded and sliced

300 g/10 oz. cooked peeled prawns/shrimp

a small bunch of fresh coriander/cilantro

sea salt and freshly ground black pepper

salad leaves, to serve (optional)

Serves 4–6

Ceviche is a South American dish of fish marinated in lime juice. The acid in the lime juice turns the fish opaque and changes its texture, making it seem cooked. It goes without saying that you should use the very freshest fish available – sole, snapper, tilapia and bass are all good. Serve with plenty of crusty bread to soak up the dressing.

Cut the fish into strips or chunks. Sprinkle half the onion in a glass dish and put the fish on top, sprinkling half the chilli and the ginger over the top. Pour in the juice of 5 of the limes, cover and leave to marinate in the refrigerator for 1–1½ hours, spooning the juice over the fish once or twice.

Meanwhile, put the remaining onion in a sieve/strainer and pour over a kettle of boiling water. Drain thoroughly, then put in a non-metallic bowl and toss with 1 tablespoon of the remaining lime juice, ½ teaspoon sugar and the ground coriander seeds. Cover and let stand for 20–30 minutes, tossing once or twice.

Put the oil in a small bowl and whisk in the liquid from the onions. Add salt and pepper to taste, then whisk in the lime zest. Adjust the seasoning with extra lime juice or sugar to taste. Drain the liquid from the fish and discard the onion, ginger and chilli. In a large serving bowl, toss the fish, marinated onion, avocado, papaya, prawns/shrimp and dressing. Finely chop half the fresh coriander/cilantro and mix into the ceviche.

Put a pile of salad leaves, if using, on each serving plate and spoon over the ceviche, sprinkle with the remaining coriander/cilantro leaves and the remaining chilli, then serve.

700 g/1½ lbs. cleaned small squid

1 tablespoon groundnut oil

a pinch of dried red chilli/hot pepper flakes

a handful of peppery salad leaves, such as mizuna, baby red mustard or wild rocket/arugula

2 carrots, cut into matchsticks

100 g/4 oz. mangetout/snow peas, finely shredded

1 small red onion, halved and very thinly sliced

sea salt and freshly ground black pepper

Lime, chilli and garlic dressing

2 garlic cloves

1 small red fresh chilli, deseeded and thinly sliced

1–2 teaspoons light brown muscovado sugar

3–4 tablespoons freshly squeezed lime juice

1–2 tablespoons Thai fish sauce

To serve

4 shallots, thinly sliced

vegetable oil, for shallow-frying

leaves from a small bunch of coriander/cilantro

a few mint or Thai basil leaves, torn

1 mild red fresh chilli, thinly sliced

Serves 4

It's the dressing that is the star of the show here – garlicky and at once sour with lime, sweet with brown sugar and salty with the deeply savoury flavour of Thai fish sauce. You can use this dressing on all kinds of ingredients – on shredded cold chicken or pork, or on strips of hot, seared steak, for instance.

squid salad

To prepare the squid, cut off the tentacles in one piece. Open the body to make a rough rectangle and score it lightly with a cross-hatch of cuts. Toss the squid with the oil, chilli/hot pepper flakes and a little salt. Cover and leave to marinate in the refrigerator.

Meanwhile, to make the dressing, crush the garlic with a pinch of salt in a mortar and pestle, then work in the chilli, pounding it lightly. Gradually work in 1 teaspoon sugar, 3 tablespoons lime juice and 1 tablespoon fish sauce, then let stand for 10 minutes. Add more sugar, lime juice or fish sauce, to taste.

Put the shallots in a sieve/strainer. Sprinkle with 1 teaspoon salt, leave for 30 minutes, drain in the sink, then rinse and dry on paper towels. Heat a shallow layer of oil in a small frying pan/skillet set over medium heat and cook the shallots gently until golden brown and crisp. Drain on paper towels.

Heat a ridged stove-top grill pan until very hot. Add the squid and sear very quickly for 1 minute on each side. The squid will curl and turn opaque and brown in places. Arrange the salad leaves on serving plates and sprinkle with half the coriander/cilantro leaves. Toss the vegetables with about 2 tablespoons of the dressing, then arrange on the salad leaves. Add the squid, then finish the salad with the remaining coriander/cilantro, the mint leaves, the crisp-fried shallots and chilli. Finally, sprinkle with the remaining dressing and serve immediately.

1 tablespoon peanut oil

1 tablespoon red Thai curry paste

12 uncooked prawns/shrimp, shelled, deveined and halved lengthways

12 cherry tomatoes, halved

a handful of mint sprigs, to serve

Spicy thai dressing

1 stalk of lemongrass, outer leaves discarded, remainder very finely chopped

2 fresh red bird's eye chillies, finely sliced and deseeded

2 pink Thai shallots or 1 small regular shallot, finely sliced lengthways

1 tablespoon brown sugar or palm sugar

freshly squeezed juice and finely grated zest of 2 limes

a handful of coriander/cilantro leaves, finely chopped

3 spring onions/scallions, finely chopped

2 kaffir lime leaves, mid-rib removed, the leaves very finely sliced crossways, then finely chopped

Serves 4

spicy thai seafood salad

This salad is very easy to make but to simplify it further you can use pre-cooked prawns/shrimp. When preparing the lemongrass and kaffir lime leaves, make sure to slice them very finely indeed. If you can't find them, use a squeeze of lemon juice and some extra grated regular lime zest instead.

Heat the oil and curry paste in a wok, add the prawns/shrimp and stir-fry for about 1 minute until opaque. Let cool.

To make the dressing, crush the lemongrass, 1 chilli and half the shallots with a mortar and pestle. Add the sugar, lime juice and zest and mix well until the sugar dissolves. Stir in the remaining chilli and shallots, and the coriander/cilantro, spring onions/scallions and lime leaves.

Put the prawns/shrimp into a serving bowl, add the cherry tomatoes, pour the dressing over the top and toss well. Serve, topped with mint.

Variation

Use scallops instead of prawns/shrimp. Prick the corals with a toothpick before cooking or they will explode in the heat.

Salads with starchy carbohydrates are most often served as side dishes, but the recipes here make good use of fresh and colourful ingredients to create robust salads – perfect for lunchboxes, picnics and speedy midweek meals.

pasta, noodles and potato

niçoise pasta salad

This classic combination of salty tuna and olives, crunchy beans, refreshing tomato and creamy egg works well in this simple yet filling pasta salad.

40 g/1 cup wholemeal pasta spirals or shells

125 g/5 oz. green beans, halved

1 egg (optional)

50 g/¼ cup pitted black olives

200-g/8-oz. can of tuna steak in spring water or oil, as preferred, drained and flaked

100 g/4 oz. cherry tomatoes, halved

2 Little Gem lettuces, leaves separated

Dressing

1 tablespoon freshly squeezed lemon juice

1 tablespoon extra virgin olive oil

1 small garlic clove, crushed

2 tablespoons chopped basil

sea salt and freshly ground black pepper

Serves 2

Cook the pasta in a large saucepan of lightly salted boiling water for about 12 minutes, until tender. Add the green beans to the pan for the last 3 minutes of cooking time. Drain the pasta and beans, then refresh briefly with cold water.

Meanwhile, add the egg to a small saucepan of cold water. Bring to the boil, then simmer for 6 minutes. Drain and rinse under cold water until cool. Peel the egg and cut in half.

Whisk the dressing ingredients together with the seasoning in a mixing bowl. Mix in the pasta and beans, olives, flaked tuna and cherry tomatoes. Divide the lettuce leaves between serving bowls and top with the pasta and the hard-boiled egg halves. Serve immediately.

pea, prosciutto and pasta salad

This is an elegant and light twist on a traditional pasta salad. You can either use frozen peas or make the most of the tender sweetness of fresh peas when they are in season.

350 g/12 oz. pasta shape of your choice, such as orecchiette, fusilli or farfalle

1 tablespoon olive oil

1 large onion, finely chopped

2 garlic cloves, crushed

100 g/4 oz. sliced prosciutto or bacon rashers

350 g/2 cups frozen or fresh peas

2 tablespoons extra virgin olive oil

2 tablespoons white wine vinegar

1 teaspoon Dijon mustard

2 tablespoons chopped parsley

2 tablespoons chopped chervil

2 tablespoons chopped mint

sea salt and freshly ground black pepper

Serves 6

Bring a large saucepan of water to the boil, add plenty of salt and return to the boil. Cook the pasta according to the packet instructions.

While the pasta is cooking, heat the olive oil in a frying pan/ skillet set over medium heat. Add the onion and garlic and cook for 5 minutes. Add the prosciutto and cook a further 5 minutes. Add the peas, cover and cook gently for 5 minutes until the peas are tender. (Remember that fresh peas will need slightly less cooking time.)

In a bowl, mix together the extra virgin olive oil, vinegar and mustard, adding salt and pepper to taste.

When the pasta is cooked, drain and refresh with cold water to cool a little. Combine the pasta with the pea and prosciutto mixture, vinaigrette, parsley, chervil and mint.

500 ml/2 cups chicken stock

250 ml/1 cup dry white wine

1 small onion, sliced

1 celery rib, cut into 3 pieces

1 bay leaf

2 slices of lemon

8–10 black peppercorns

4 skinless, boneless chicken breasts

200 g/8 oz. dried pasta shapes

8 halved, grilled artichoke hearts

1 tablespoon chopped flat-leaf parsley

500 g/l lb. cherry tomatoes

For the dressing

100-g/4-oz jar of premium tuna

2 tablespoons small capers, rinsed

2 tablespoons freshly squeezed lemon juice

3 jarred anchovy fillets, rinsed and finely chopped

200 g/1 cup mayonnaise

a pinch of cayenne pepper

For the gremolata

5–6 jarred anchovy fillets, rinsed and chopped

2 spring onions/scallions, sliced

grated zest of 1 small lemon

1 tablespoon small capers

3 tablespoons chopped flat-leaf parsley

Serves 6

This is a really easy yet impressive pasta salad. Don't be daunted by the rather long list of ingredients – the gremolata is based on pretty well the same ingredients as the dressing, but simply chopped rough for added texture.

chicken tonnato pasta salad

Pour the stock and wine into a large saucepan, big enough to take the chicken breasts in a single layer. Bring to the boil, add the onion, celery, bay leaf, lemon and peppercorns and simmer for 5 minutes. Carefully lower the chicken breasts into the stock, adding some boiling water, if needed, to cover them. Bring back to the boil, then turn the heat right down and simmer very slowly for another 5 minutes. Turn the heat off, cover the pan and let the chicken cool in the stock. (This will take about 4–5 hours.)

Once the chicken is cool, make the dressing. Put the drained tuna in a food processor with the capers, lemon juice and anchovy fillets and whizz until you have a paste. Add the mayonnaise and cayenne pepper and whizz again until smooth. Turn into a large bowl. Put all the ingredients for the gremolata on a chopping board and chop them together.

Cook the pasta following the instructions on the packet and refresh with cold water.

Remove the chicken from the poaching liquid and cut into rough chunks. Add the chicken, pasta and gremolata to the dressing and toss lightly. Check the seasoning, adding more lemon juice or cayenne pepper to taste if you think it needs it (you shouldn't need salt). Spoon onto serving plates, arrange the artichoke hearts over the top and sprinkle with parsley just before serving.

200 g/7 oz. rice stick noodles

1 tablespoon groundnut oil

3 carrots, peeled

200 g/7 oz. Savoy or Chinese cabbage, very thinly sliced

6 radishes, thinly sliced

3 spring onions/scallions, thinly sliced lengthways

100 g/4 oz. water chestnuts, thinly sliced

70 g/¼ cup cashew nuts or almonds, toasted and roughly chopped

Chinese five-spice dressing

1 tablespoon sugar

½ teaspoon crushed fresh red chilli

½ teaspoon Chinese five-spice powder

2 tablespoons Japanese soy sauce

2 tablespoons rice vinegar

1 tablespoon freshly squeezed lime or lemon juice

1 teaspoon sesame oil

Serves 4–6

rice noodle, carrot and cabbage salad with chinese five-spice dressing

This is a spicy twist on a traditional coleslaw. To turn it into a substantial meal, simply toss through cooked and sliced chicken or pork or fried tofu.

Put the rice stick noodles in a heatproof bowl and cover with boiling water. Leave for 5 minutes or until soft, then drain well. Toss with the groundnut oil to stop the noodles sticking together.

To make the Chinese five-spice dressing, combine the sugar, chilli, five-spice powder, soy sauce, vinegar, lime juice and sesame oil in a small bowl. Stir until the sugar has dissolved.

Cut the carrots into thin ribbons – this can be done using a mandoline if you have one or a vegetable peeler. Put in a large bowl with the noodles, cabbage, radishes, spring onions/scallions and water chestnuts. Add the dressing and toss to mix.

Transfer to serving dishes and scatter with the toasted nuts to serve.

lobster noodle salad with fresh coconut and fruit

This is an exotic salad that can be found in South-east Asia. Fresh coconuts aren't always available, but if you see them for sale buy one and try this salad.

200 g/7 oz. dried beanthread noodles

2 medium cooked lobsters

2 fresh coconuts

Dressing

1 tablespoon palm sugar or soft brown sugar

freshly squeezed juice of 4 limes

1 teaspoon freshly ground green bell pepper

½ teaspoon sea salt

2 tablespoons peanut oil

To serve

1 fresh starfruit, thinly sliced

2 tablespoons chopped coriander/cilantro

2 tablespoons chopped mint

2 tablespoons dry roasted peanuts, coarsely chopped, plus extra to serve (optional)

Serves 4

Put the noodles into a bowl, cover with very hot water and let soak for 10 minutes or until soft. Drain, rinse under cold running water and drain again. Chop into 5-cm/2-inch lengths with kitchen shears and set aside.

Remove the flesh from the cooked lobsters and shred it finely.

Crack open the coconuts and scoop out the white flesh. Using a fork, shred the coconut flesh into small strips.

Put the dressing ingredients into a bowl and stir well to dissolve the sugar.

Put the noodles into a large bowl, add the lobster and coconut, pour the dressing over the top and stir gently.

Transfer to serving plates, arrange the starfruit slices on top, then add the coriander/cilantro, mint and peanuts. Serve extra peanuts separately, if using.

500 g/l lb. any noodles

1 tablespoon sesame oil

Peanut noodle sauce

1 teaspoon Szechuan peppercorns

3-cm/2-inch piece of fresh ginger, peeled and coarsely chopped

2 large juicy garlic cloves

4 tablespoons smooth peanut butter

4 tablespoons soy sauce

3 teaspoons chilli-infused oil

½ teaspoon sea salt

2 teaspoons caster sugar

6 spring onions/scallions, finely sliced diagonally

3 tablespoons raw peanuts, toasted and coarsely chopped

Serves 4

This is a great prepare-ahead dish for a crowd. You can use any type of Oriental noodle for this; there are so many available today – some dried, some ready-to-use. Even Italian pasta works well with this delicious peanut sauce!

cold noodle salad with peanut sauce

Cook the noodles according to the packet instructions, depending on type. Drain, rinse well and let drain for a couple of minutes. Add a little sesame oil and toss gently.

Heat a small frying pan/skillet and toast the Szechuan peppercorns for a couple of minutes until they smell aromatic and begin to smoke a little. Do not let them burn. Tip into a bowl and let cool. Grind to a powder using a pepper grinder or in mortar and pestle.

Transfer to a food processor, add the ginger, garlic, peanut butter, soy sauce, chilli oil, salt, sugar and 140 ml/generous ½ cup warm water and blend until smooth and creamy. Beat in extra warm water if too thick. Add the sauce to the noodles, toss well, then transfer to serving dishes and sprinkle the spring onions/scallions and peanuts on top.

new potato, crisp salami and sesame salad

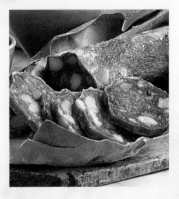

The perfect accompaniment to grilled food, potato salad is essential summer fare. This version makes a change from the usual, looks stunning and is packed with flavour, making it great for those bring-a-plate occasions. If time is short, you can use good-quality bought mayonnaise combined with a squeeze of lemon juice.

800 g/1¾ lbs. waxy new potatoes

a pinch of sea salt

2 tablespoons sesame seeds

150 g/6 oz. thinly sliced salami (a fatty, unflavoured variety)

½ quantity lemon mayonnaise (see below)

75 g/3 oz. rocket/arugula

a small bunch of dill, chopped

Lemon mayonnaise

1 egg yolk, at room temperature

2 tablespoons freshly squeezed lemon juice

a pinch of sea salt

125 ml/½ cup plain-flavoured oil, such as grape seed

1 teaspoon sesame oil

Serves 6

To make the lemon mayonnaise, put the egg yolk, half the lemon juice and salt in a bowl. Whisk to mix. While whisking continuously, slowly add the plain-flavoured oil a drop at a time until fully incorporated. Whisk in the sesame oil and remaining lemon juice. Cover and set aside until needed. (Note that this recipe makes approximately double the quantity required for this salad. The remainder will keep in the refrigerator for up to 3 days.)

If necessary, cut the potatoes into even-sized pieces. Put in a large saucepan. Cover with cold water, add the salt, bring to the boil, then simmer until tender. Drain and set aside.

Heat a frying pan/skillet to medium heat, add the sesame seeds and toast for about 6–8 minutes, stirring until golden. Set aside.

Reheat the frying pan/skillet until hot, add the salami slices and cook for a few minutes on each side until browned. Remove and drain on paper towels. (It will crisp up more as it cools.)

Arrange the rocket/arugula in a serving bowl. Toss the potatoes with the lemon mayonnaise and pile on top of the rocket/arugula. Scatter with half the toasted sesame seeds and dill. Crumble over the crisp salami and scatter with the remaining sesame seeds and dill to serve.

saffron potato salad with sun-dried tomatoes and caper and basil dressing

500 g/1 lb. large waxy yellow-fleshed potatoes, peeled

a pinch of saffron threads

8 sun-dried tomatoes (the dry kind, not in oil)

Caper and basil dressing

6 tablespoons extra virgin olive oil

3 tablespoons chopped basil leaves, plus extra to serve

2 tablespoons salted capers, rinsed and chopped, if large

1–2 tablespoons freshly squeezed lemon juice, to taste

sea salt and freshly ground black pepper

Serves 4

The potatoes absorb the glorious golden colour and subtle flavour of the saffron as they simmer gently with the tomatoes. Serve this warm, as the heat will release the heady aromas of the basil and saffron.

Cut the potatoes into large chunks. Put in a saucepan, add enough cold water to just cover them, then add the saffron and sun-dried tomatoes. Bring slowly to the boil, then turn down the heat, cover and simmer very gently for about 12 minutes until just tender. If the water boils too fast, the potatoes will start to disintegrate. Drain well.

Pick out the now plumped up sun-dried tomatoes and slice them thinly. Tip the potatoes into a large bowl and add the sliced tomatoes.

To make the dressing, put the oil, chopped basil and capers in a small bowl. Add lemon juice, salt and pepper to taste and mix well. Pour over the hot potatoes, mix gently, then serve hot or warm, scattered with extra basil leaves.

Texture plays a big part in making or breaking a good salad. Both cheese and nuts make superb additions for this reason and also add a welcome depth of flavour. These salads make particularly good first courses as they are both stylish and fuss-free.

nuts and cheese

roasted sweet potato and macadamia nut salad

3 sweet potatoes (about 300 g/10 oz. each), peeled

1 tablespoon olive oil

1 teaspoon sea salt flakes

70 g/⅓ cup raw macadamia nuts, roughly chopped

200 g/7 oz. baby spinach leaves, washed

Macadamia nut dressing

1 tablespoon cider vinegar

1 teaspoon wholegrain mustard

2 tablespoons macadamia nut oil

sea salt and freshly ground black pepper

Serves 4

Macadamia nuts add a great crunch to this salad, but can be replaced by any other nuts or even toasted sunflower or pumpkin seeds if you prefer.

Preheat the oven to 190°C (375°F) Gas 5.

Cut the sweet potatoes into 2-cm/1-inch cubes and toss in a bowl with the olive oil and salt flakes. Tip onto a baking sheet and roast in the preheated oven for 10 minutes.

Put the macadamia nuts in the bowl and toss with any residual oil. Add to the sweet potatoes and roast in the hot oven for 10 minutes, giving the sweet potatoes 20 minutes in total.

To make the dressing, mix together the vinegar, mustard and macadamia oil or olive in a small bowl. Season to taste with salt and pepper.

Arrange the spinach leaves on serving plates and top with the sweet potatoes and macadamia nuts. Drizzle or spoon the dressing over the top and serve immediately.

This salad is all about texture and taste with the added bonus of being simple to prepare and looking stunning. Micro greens look great and have a delicate sweet flavour, but alfalfa or broccoli sprouts are also good.

iceberg, blue cheese and date salad with saffron and walnut dressing

1 iceberg lettuce

200 g/7 oz. creamy blue cheese

8 dried medjool dates

70 g/½ cup walnut halves

a large handful of micro greens (sprouts)

Saffron and walnut dressing

½ teaspoon saffron threads

2 tablespoons freshly squeezed orange juice

1 tablespoon white wine vinegar

½ teaspoon sea salt

6 tablespoons walnut oil

Serves 6

To make the saffron and walnut dressing, put the saffron and orange juice in a bowl and leave to infuse for about 10 minutes. Whisk in the vinegar and salt, then the oil, whisking continuously. Cover and set aside until needed.

Slice the lettuce into 8 wedges, then cut each wedge into 3 pieces, giving you a total of 24 pieces. Arrange them in a serving bowl.

Cut the cheese into pieces and arrange these among the lettuce. Chop the dates into 4 and discard the pits. Scatter them over the lettuce along with the walnuts. Pour over the dressing, then scatter over the micro greens. Serve immediately.

600 g/1 ¼ lbs. small courgettes/baby zucchini

¼ teaspoon dried red chilli/hot pepper flakes

1 tablespoon extra virgin olive oil

200 g/7 oz. feta cheese, crumbled

4 tablespoons toasted pine nuts

Lemon, caper and mint dressing

4 tablespoons extra virgin olive oil

1 tablespoon freshly squeezed lemon juice

½ teaspoon balsamic vinegar, plus extra to taste

½ teaspoon grated lemon zest

1–2 garlic cloves, finely chopped

1 tablespoon chopped mint, plus a few whole leaves to garnish

2 tablespoons chopped flat-leaf parsley

2 tablespoons small salted capers, rinsed and soaked in cold water for 10 minutes, then drained

sea salt and freshly ground black pepper

Serves 4–6

grilled courgette and feta salad with lemon, caper and mint dressing

This is based on a classic southern Italian way of cooking courgettes/zucchini. It makes a lovely first course, either alone or as part of a mixed antipasti. Alternatively, serve it as an accompaniment to a simply grilled lamb steak.

Cut the courgettes/zucchini lengthways into fine slices. Put in a colander and toss with 1 teaspoon salt. Leave for 30–60 minutes to drain in the sink, then rinse and dry on paper towels.

Season with lots of pepper and the chilli/hot pepper flakes, if using. Add the oil and toss to coat. Heat a ridged stove-top grill pan until hot and grill the courgettes/zucchini for 6–8 minutes, turning once, until well browned and just tender. Alternatively, heat a grill/broiler to hot, put them on a baking sheet and grill/broil for 6–8 minutes, turning once. Transfer to a dish.

To make the dressing, put the oil, lemon juice, balsamic vinegar, lemon zest, garlic and chopped mint and parsley in a bowl and whisk well. Stir in the capers and pour the dressing over the courgettes. Cover and set aside for 30–60 minutes for the flavours to marry. Just before serving, mix in the feta cheese and serve sprinkled with the pine nuts and a few mint leaves.

winter-spiced salad with pears, honeyed pecans and ricotta

1 star anise

1 cinnamon stick

2 pears, unpeeled, quartered and cored

150 g/5–6 oz. prepared salad leaves, such as rocket/arugula or shredded radicchio

125 g/4–5 oz. buffalo ricotta

Honeyed pecans

50 g/½ cup pecans

¼ teaspoon dried chilli/hot pepper flakes

¼ teaspoon fennel seeds

3 tablespoons runny honey

Dressing

4 tablespoons sunflower oil

1 tablespoon walnut oil

freshly squeezed juice of 1 lemon

1 large red fresh chilli, partly deseeded and chopped

Serves 4

You need to be careful when buying ricotta because it can sometimes be very soggy, especially when sold in tubs. Organic varieties or buffalo ricotta are crumbly rather than creamy, which is what you need here. Buffalo mozzarella also works well, as does a soft, fresh goats' cheese.

Fill a large saucepan with water and add the star anise and cinnamon stick. Bring to the boil and add the pears. Poach for 12 minutes, or until tender.

Put the pecans, a large pinch of salt, the chilli/hot pepper flakes and the fennel seeds in a frying pan/skillet and toast until golden and aromatic. Pour in the honey, turn the heat right up and leave to bubble away for a few minutes. Tip onto parchment paper and leave to cool.

Meanwhile, to make the dressing, whisk together the sunflower and walnut oils, the lemon juice and chilli.

Transfer the salad leaves to serving bowls, scatter over the pears and crumble over the ricotta. Drizzle with the dressing. Roughly break up the nuts with your fingers and scatter them over the top.

Roasting beetroot takes time, but it is worth it for the resulting wonderfully sweet flavour. If you have a outdoor grill going, try wrapping the beetroot in foil and baking them in the embers. The feta can be replaced with grilled halloumi if preferred.

roast beetroot, orange and feta salad

600 g/1¼ lbs. baby or small beetroot/beets, unpeeled and trimmed

1 red onion

a large handful of crisp salad leaves

3 oranges

150 g/1 cup walnuts or hazelnuts

200 g/7 oz. feta cheese, cubed

a small bunch of flat-leaf parsley, roughly chopped

micro greens (sprouts), to garnish (optional)

Honey cider vinaigrette

1 tablespoon runny honey

½ teaspoon sea salt

¼ teaspoon white pepper

2 tablespoons cider vinegar

4 tablespoons olive oil

Serves 4

Preheat the oven to 180°C (350°F) Gas 4.

To make the honey cider vinaigette, combine the honey, salt, pepper and vinegar in a small bowl and whisk in the oil. Set aside.

Put the unpeeled beetroot/beets on a baking sheet and bake in the preheated oven until tender – about 30 minutes for baby beets, 45 minutes for small beets. Remove from the oven and let cool. When cool enough to handle, peel off the skins – they should come away easily in your fingers. Trim the ends and discard. Cut the beetroot in half if necessary and toss with a little of the honey cider vinaigrette. Set aside.

Slice the onion very finely, using a mandoline if you have one. Put in a bowl of iced water for 10 minutes. Drain well.

Put the salad leaves on a serving platter. With a sharp knife, remove the rind and all the white pith from the oranges. Slice and arrange on top of the salad leaves.

Heat a frying pan/skillet, add the walnuts and toast for a couple of minutes until browned. Scatter these over the leaves and oranges with the beetroot and onion. Drizzle over the honey cider vinaigrette. Scatter the feta over the salad and sprinkle with the parsley and micro greens, if using. Serve immediately.

cheese, apple and hazelnut salad

2 tablespoons shelled hazelnuts

1 tablespoon sunflower oil

100 g/5 oz. smoked bacon lardons or pancetta cubes

1 Little Gem lettuce, leaves separated

75 g/4 oz. smoked chicken, torn into strips

60 g/3 oz. semi-hard cheese such as Comté or Gruyère, thinly sliced on the diagonal

1 eating apple, such as Cox or Blenheim, quartered, cored and cut into wedges

a few root vegetable crisps

a small handful of fresh chives, snipped

Dressing

2 tablespoons crab apple jelly, rowan jelly or redcurrant jelly

2 tablespoons pure apple juice

1 teaspoon cider vinegar

sea salt and freshly ground black pepper

Serves 2

Here is an attractive salad, perfect for winter entertaining and substantial enough to serve as a main course.

Preheat the oven to 180°C (350°F) Gas 4.

Put the hazelnuts on a baking sheet and roast in the preheated oven for 10 minutes, or until the skins turn dark brown. Leave to cool for a few minutes, then tip them onto a clean kitchen towel and rub off the skins. Cut the hazelnuts in half.

Heat the oil in a frying pan/skillet and fry the bacon until crisp. Take the pan off the heat, remove the bacon from the pan with a slotted spoon and transfer to a plate lined with paper towels. Pour off all but 1 tablespoon of the fat, add the crab apple jelly for the dressing and stir until melted, putting the pan back on the heat if necessary. Add the apple juice and cider vinegar and a splash of water if needed to thin the dressing. Season with salt and pepper and set aside.

Take serving plates and arrange the lettuce leaves on each plate. Top with the bacon and smoked chicken, then the cheese and apple. Drizzle over the dressing and scatter with the hazelnuts, a few root vegetable crisps and the chives. Serve the remaining root vegetable crisps in a bowl alongside.

sweet curried salad of cheese and greens

½–1 teaspoon curry powder,
to taste

2 tablespoons mango chutney

4 tablespoons mayonnaise

1 tablespoon cider vinegar

¼ teaspoon sea salt

2 small leeks

3 celery ribs, sliced

½ iceberg lettuce, sliced

a bunch of chives, chopped

70 g/½ cup cashew nuts, roasted
and chopped

150 g/6 oz, mild cheese, such as
Edam or Colby

½ teaspoon nigella seeds

warm bread, to serve

Serves 4

This unusual combination is a total mishmash of cuisines,
but somehow works brilliantly and tastes fantastic served
with warmed Indian-style bread such as naan. You could
substitute the cheese for cooked chicken if you prefer.

In a bowl, whisk together ½ teaspoon of the curry powder, the
chutney, mayonnaise, vinegar and salt. Taste and add more curry
powder if liked. Set aside.

Wash the leeks thoroughly and slice as thinly as you can. Either
use the leeks raw (as I like to) or blanch them in boiling water
if you prefer a milder flavour. Place in a serving bowl with the
celery, lettuce, chives and cashew nuts.

Cut the cheese into 1-cm/½-inch cubes and add to the salad.
Pour in the dressing and mix well.

Heat a frying pan/skillet over medium heat, add the nigella
seeds and toast, tossing in the pan, for about 1 minute until
just fragrant.

Sprinkle the nigella seeds over the salad. Serve immediately
with plenty of warm bread.

The recipes in this chapter make use of so-called 'superfood' ingredients, such as seeds and beans, sprouted grains, dried and fresh fruits, raw vegetables and even seaweed! They pack a powerful nutritional punch without sacrificing on flavour.

superfood salads

mineral-boost salad

4 strips of dried wakame

20 g/½ cup dried dulse

20 g/½ cup dried arame

1 sheet of dried nori

2 cucumbers

2 large carrots

100 g/1 cup shredded red cabbage

25 g/¼ cup chopped spring onions/scallions

50 g/½ cup fresh flat-leaf parsley leaves, chopped

Dressing

2 tablespoons umeboshi vinegar

2 tablespoons tamari soy sauce, or to taste

4 tablespoons rice or apple cider vinegar, or to taste

4 tablespoons flaxseed oil

Serves 4

There are no other vegetables that are simultaneously as precious and as neglected as sea vegetables. However, they offer one of the broadest ranges of minerals of any food, and no existing mineral supplements can compete with them, since seaweed minerals are so much more easily recognized and absorbed by our bodies.

Put each seaweed in a separate bowl and cover with warm water. Allow to soak until soft.

Drain all the seaweed well. Cut the wakame and dulse into thin strips. Peel and dice the cucumbers. Peel the carrots and cut into thin matchsticks.

Combine all the vegetables, the cabbage, wakame, dulse and arame in a salad bowl.

For the vinaigrette, put all the ingredients in a small jar, seal tightly and shake to emulsify the ingredients.

Alternatively, put the ingredients in a small bowl and whisk gently to combine.

Pour the vinaigrette over the salad, mix gently and allow to stand for 15 minutes, or until the vegetables have wilted slightly.

Cut the nori into strips and scatter on top of the salad just before serving.

powerhouse salad

2 handfuls of wild rocket/arugula

a handful of baby spinach leaves

a handful of radicchio

5 tablespoons fresh sweetcorn/corn kernels

2 tablespoons alfalfa sprouts

1 red grapefruit, peeled and divided into segments

2 tablespoons cured black olives, such as kalamata or niçoise, pitted

3 tablespoons walnut halves

1 tablespoon sunflower seeds

1 teaspoon chia seeds

Avocado dressing

1 ripe avocado, peeled and pitted

2 tablespoons umeboshi vinegar

freshly squeezed lemon juice, to taste

freshly ground black pepper

Serves 2–3

This amazing bowl of goodness is packed full of nutrients. Walnuts, sunflower seeds and avocado dressing give you plenty of energy; alfalfa sprouts, grapefruit and greens will add a touch of freshness; and olives will bring a salty taste to this tasty and colourful salad.

Put all the salad ingredients in a large bowl and toss gently to combine.

To make the dressing, put the ingredients in a food processor and blend until smooth, adding a little water if needed. Season with black pepper.

Divide the salad between 2–3 chilled serving bowls and drizzle the dressing on top and serve immediately.

10 baby carrots, scrubbed and thinly sliced

125 g/1 cup peas, fresh from their pods

125 g/1 cup raw sweetcorn/corn kernels

80 g/1 cup pomegranate seeds

120 g/1 cup pine nuts

4 tablespoons salt-cured capers

4 tablespoons flaxseed oil

2 tablespoons tamari soy sauce

2 tablespoons freshly squeezed lemon juice

Parsley dressing

50 g/1 cup fresh flat-leaf parsley leaves, chopped

2 garlic cloves, crushed

4 tablespoons rice vinegar, or other vinegar

60 ml/¼ cup virgin olive oil

finely grated zest of 1 lemon

4 tablespoons black sesame seeds

sea salt and freshly ground black pepper

Serves 4

This salad is inspired by the sorts of vegetables, nuts and seeds that resemble little gems. When combined to make a salad, they create a visually striking effect. Bright colours, a wealth of flavours and a satisfying crunchiness will make every mouthful a delight!

micro salad with parsley dressing

Put all the salad ingredients in a large bowl, mix and allow to stand while you make the parsley dressing.

To make the parsley dressing, put all the ingredients except the sesame seeds in a small jar, seal tightly and shake to emulsify the ingredients. Alternatively, put the ingredients in a small bowl and whisk gently to combine. Add a little water if needed. Season with salt and pepper to taste.

Pour the dressing over the salad and sprinkle the sesame seeds over the top. Serve immediately.

flower-power salad

200 g/5 cups mixed salad leaves

2 ripe avocados, cubed

50 g/1 cup shredded radicchio

8 calendula flowers

4 tablespoons chive blossoms

4 tablespoons basil flowers

2 tablespoons rosemary blossoms

30 g/¼ cup dried cranberries

Power dressing

150 g/1 cup macadamia nuts

60 g/½ cup grated celery or parsnip

1 small onion, grated

1 tablespoon nutritional yeast (optional)

freshly squeezed lemon juice, to taste

sea salt

Serves 4

Flowers give a touch of elegance to a meal and their delicate taste is unique. Use them sparingly, don't harvest them by the roadside, make sure they have not been treated in any way and eat them only when you are sure they are edible!

For the dressing, put the macadamia nuts, celery or parsnip and onion in a food processor with a little water and blitz to get a smooth dressing. Add the yeast, if using, and lemon juice and salt to taste. Blitz again until smooth.

Put the salad leaves, avocados and radicchio in a salad bowl and mix. Divide between 4 bowls and sprinkle the flowers and cranberries equally over each portion. Serve with the dressing on the side.

red salad with beetroot, red cabbage and harissa dressing

6–8 small beetroot/beets

2–4 small whole heads of garlic, preferably pink spring garlic

olive oil, for roasting

1 small red cabbage

2 tablespoons white wine vinegar, cider vinegar or lemon juice

2 red onions, very finely sliced

1 tablespoon umiboshi vinegar

sea salt and freshly ground black pepper

2 medium fresh red chillies, very finely sliced

Harissa dressing

125 ml/½ cup extra virgin olive oil

1 tablespoon harissa paste

Serves 4–6

This is a variation on a red coleslaw, but the addition of beetroot makes an appealing colour combination. Crushing the cabbage with your hands, breaks its fibres and releases its delicious juices.

Preheat the oven to 200°C (400°F) Gas 6.

Leave the beetroot/beets whole and unpeeled. Cut the top off each garlic, about 1 cm/½ inch from the stalk. Put the beetroot and garlic in a small baking dish, add olive oil, turn to coat, then season with salt and pepper. Roast in the preheated oven for about 30–45 minutes or until the beetroot and garlic are tender (you may have to remove the beetroot first). When cooked, remove from the oven and cut the beetroot into 4 wedges.

About 15 minutes before the beetroot are cooked, cut the cabbage in quarters and remove the white cores. Cut the quarters into fine slices and put in a bowl. Sprinkle with vinegar and turn and mash the cabbage with your hands. Put the sliced onion in a bowl and cover with boiling water. Drain just before using.

Push the roasted pulp out of 4 garlic cloves and put it in a serving bowl. Add the oil and harissa and beat with a fork. Drain the onions, pat dry with paper towels, then add to the bowl. Sprinkle with umiboshi vinegar. Add the cabbage and beetroot and toss gently. Taste and adjust the seasoning with salt and pepper and top with the chillies. Put the heads of garlic beside for people to press out the delicious flesh themselves.

Kumquats are a small, oval fruit with a strong and pleasant citrus smell. They can be eaten whole, without peeling and make a wonderful addition to summer salads. If you can't find them, substitute seedless mandarin segments.

150 g/3⅔ cups wild rocket/arugula

150 g/3 cups curly endive

10–15 kumquats

60 g/½ cup Brazil nuts, chopped

Spicy honey dressing

2 tablespoons raw honey or agave nectar

1 tablespoon chilli-infused olive oil

2 tablespoons chia seed oil

4 tablespoons freshly squeezed lemon juice

sea salt and freshly ground black pepper

Serves 4

spicy and sweet salad with kumquats and brazil nuts

Wash the rocket/arugula, endive and kumquats well. Cut the kumquats into thin slices.

For the dressing, put the honey or agave nectar, olive oil, chia seed oil and lemon juice in a small jar, seal tightly and shake to emulsify the ingredients. Alternatively, put the ingredients in a small bowl and whisk gently to combine. Add a little water if needed. Season with salt and pepper to taste.

Put the greens, kumquats and Brazil nuts in a salad bowl and add the dressing. Mix gently, then serve immediately before the greens have time to wilt.

Variations

You can replace the chilli-infused oil with a pinch of dried chilli/hot pepper flakes or chilli powder mixed in olive oil. You can also use orange instead of lemon juice. The Brazil nuts are interchangeable with any other nuts you have in the cupboards.

indonesian gado gado

a large handful of green beans, trimmed and halved

1 red or orange bell pepper

2 firm tofu cakes

plain/all-purpose flour, for dusting

2 red onions, finely sliced

a large handful of beansprouts, rinsed, drained and trimmed

1 cos/romaine lettuce heart

15-cm/6-inch daikon (mooli or white radish), peeled and cut into matchsticks

2 mini cucumbers, sliced, or 20-cm/8-inch regular cucumber, halved lengthways and sliced

½ packet prawn/shrimp crackers

peanut oil, for shallow frying

Peanut sauce

1 recipe Peanut Sauce (see page 10)

Serves 4

This tasty salad is a great way to serve tofu. It is traditionally served with all the ingredients lined up so you can take your pick of them but if everything is mixed together the flavours have a chance to infuse with delicious results.

Make the Peanut Sauce following the recipe given on page 10.

Bring a large saucepan of water to the boil and add the beans. Cook for about 1 minute, then tip into a sieve/strainer set over a bowl. Run cold water over them. When cool, transfer to a bowl of iced water. Just before serving, drain again and let dry in the colander.

Peel the pepper with a vegetable peeler. Cut off the top and bottom and remove the membranes and seeds, open out and slice thinly.

Put about 2 tablespoons of peanut oil in a frying pan/skillet, dip the tofu in flour, then add to the frying pan and fry until brown on all sides. Drain and slice thickly.

Fill a wok or saucepan two-thirds full of peanut oil and heat until a piece of noodle will puff up immediately. Add the onion and fry until crisp and golden. Remove and drain on paper towels.

Arrange all the prepared ingredients in serving bowls, drizzle with the peanut sauce, top with the onions and crackers and serve immediately.

melon, cos and cucumber salad with orange chipotle vinaigrette

A sweet, fresh salad with a tangy dressing – perfect as an accompaniment to lighter meals, such as pan-fried shellfish, fish or poultry, or on it's own as a summer appetizer.

125 g/4 oz. baby cos/romaine lettuce leaves

400-g/14-oz canteloupe melon

400-g/14-oz honeydew melon

400-g/14-oz watermelon

1 small (Lebanese) cucumber

a small bunch of coriander/cilantro

Orange chipotle vinaigrette

4 tablespoons virgin olive oil

1 chipotle chilli or 2 fresh mild red chillies plus ¼ teaspoon smoked paprika

1 tablespoon sherry vinegar or cider vinegar

finely grated zest and freshly squeezed juice of 1 orange

1 tablespoon runny honey

1 teaspoon sea salt

Serves 4–6

Arrange the lettuce on a large serving platter. Remove and discard the skin and seeds from the melons and slice the flesh into slices 1 cm/½ inch thick. Arrange these over the lettuce. Halve the cucumber lengthways and remove and discard the seeds. Slice thinly and arrange over the melon.

To make the chipotle vinaigrette, heat 1 teaspoon of the olive oil in a frying pan/skillet, add the chipotle chilli and briefly sauté for 2 minutes, stirring constantly, taking care not to let it burn.

Using kitchen shears or a sharp knife, remove the stem and seeds (leave the seeds in for extra heat if liked) from the chipotle and discard. Cut the chipotle into thin strips. If using fresh chillies, remove the stem and seeds and discard, then chop the chillies finely.

In a bowl, whisk together the vinegar, orange zest and juice, honey, salt and remaining olive oil. Add the prepared chillies and stir to combine.

Pour the vinaigrette over the lettuce, melon and cucumber on the serving platter, scatter with coriander/cilantro sprigs and serve immediately.

tomato, avocado and lime salad with crisp tortillas

freshly squeezed juice of 1 lime, plus 1 whole lime

4 ripe, firm avocados

leaves from a large bunch of coriander/cilantro

24 small tomatoes, halved

6 tablespoons olive oil or avocado oil

2 garlic cloves, crushed

2 soft flour tortillas

sea salt and freshly ground black pepper

Serves 6

Avocados are a healthy and nutritious addition to any salad and this simple Mexican-style recipe is the perfect way to enjoy them.

Put the lime juice in a bowl. Cut the avocados in half, remove the pits and peel. Cut each half into 4 wedges and toss with the lime juice.

Using a small paring knife, cut the top and bottom off of the lime. Cut away the skin and pith. Carefully slice between each segment and remove the flesh. Combine the lime flesh with the avocados, coriander/cilantro, tomatoes and 4 tablespoons of the oil. Season to taste with salt and pepper and set aside.

Preheat the grill/broiler to hot.

In a small bowl, combine the garlic and remaining 2 tablespoons of oil. Brush the oil and garlic mixture over the tortillas and toast under the preheated grill/broiler for about 1 minute until brown.

Break the toasted tortillas into pieces and scatter over the salad just before serving.

index

picture credits

Key: bg = background; ins = insert

Susan Bell
Page 6

Martin Brigdale
Pages 27, 55, 80 ins

Peter Cassidy
Pages 2, 7, 8, 9 ins, 11, 13 ins, 15, 16, 17, 19, 20, 23, 24, 28, 30, 31, 34, 35 ins, 38, 41, 42, 43 ins, 45, 46, 49, 50, 51 ins, 53, 54, 57, 58, 61, 62, 65, 72 ins, 73, 74, 77, 78, 79 bg, 79 ins, 86, 88, 92, 95, 96, 102 ins, 103, 107, 109, 110, 111 ins, 117, 121, 122, 133, 137, 138, 139 ins, 141

Tara Fisher
Pages 25 ins, 67 ins

Richard Jung
Pages 1, 3, 12, 37, 40, 67 bg, 68, 69, 70, 82, 85, 89, 98 bg, 113, 116 bg, 118

William Lingwood
Pages 32, 52, 76, 99, 120

Diana Miller
Pages 4, 104

Noel Murphy
Page 100

Steve Painter
Pages 22, 43 bg, 56, 79 bg, 116 ins

William Reavell
Pages 21, 33, 47, 66, 81, 91, 106, 114

Debi Treloar
Page 60 ins

Ian Wallace
Page 93 ins

Kate Whitaker
Pages 5, 9 bg, 10, 13 bg, 14, 18, 25 bg, 29, 32, 35 bg, 36, 39, 44, 48, 51 bg, 59, 60 bg, 63, 64, 71, 72 bg, 75, 80 bg, 83, 84, 87, 90, 93 bg, 94, 97, 98 ins, 101, 102 bg, 105, 108, 111 bg, 112, 115, 119, 123–132, 134–136, 139 bg, 140, 142-144

recipe credits

Fiona Smith
Brown rice, hazelnut and herb salad with kaffir lime dressing
Chicken, courgette/zucchini and bulghur salad with pomegranate vinaigrette
Classic Caesar salad
Classic green salad
Five-bean salad with lemon and poppy seed dressing
Greek barley salad
Green apple and wheat salad with cider mayonnaise
Herb, red onion and quinoa salad with preserved lemon
Iceberg, blue cheese and date salad with saffron and walnut dressing
Lemon-rubbed lamb and orzo salad
Melon, cos and cucumber salad with orange chipotle vinaigrette
New potato, crisp salami and sesame salad
Pea, prosciutto and pasta salad
Pickled salmon with fennel and cucumber salad
Pork and Puy lentil salad
Rice noodle, carrot and cabbage with Chinese five-spice dressing
Roast beetroot, orange and feta salad with honey cider vinaigrette
Roast duck, sausage, sweet potato and cherry salad
Roasted sweet potato and macadamia nut salad
Salad Niçoise with fresh tuna
Summer vegetables with polenta-crumbed aubergine/eggplant
Sweet curried salad of cheese and greens
Tomato, avocado and lime salad with crisp tortillas
Tuna and cannelloni bean salad
Twice-marinated beef, asparagus, pepper and bean salad

Elsa Petersen-Schepelern
Black rice salad with chilli greens
Cobb salad
Indonesian gado gado
Insalata Caprese
Lobster noodle salad with fresh coconut and fruit
Puy lentil salad
Quick chickpea salad

Red salad with beetroot/beet, red cabbage and harissa dressing
Spicy Thai prawn/shrimp salad
Thai mango beef salad
Vietnamese duck salad
Waldorf salad

Dunja Gulin
Flower power salad
Micro salad with parsley dressing
Mineral boost salad
Powerhouse salad
Spicy and sweet salad with Kumquats and brazil nuts

Fiona Beckett
Cheese, apple and hazelnut salad
Chicken tonnato

Tamsin Burnett-Hall
Nicoise pasta salad
Smoked mackerel and bulghur wheat salad

Maxine Clark
Cold noodles with peanut sauce
Saffron potato salad

Liz Franklin
Bang-bang chicken salad
Marinated chicken, raisin and chilli salad with hazelnut dressing

Tonia George
Couscous with feta, dill and spring beans
Thai chicken larb
Winter-spiced salad with pears, honeyed pecans and ricotta

Brian Glover
Ceviche
Grilled courgette/zucchini and feta salad with lemon, caper and mint dressing
Rice salad with preserved lemon dressing
Squid salad